A HOME COMPANION

My year of living like my grandmother

Wendyl Nissen

ALLEN&UNWIN

This edition published in 2011
First published in 2010

Other books by Wendyl Nissen
Bitch and Famous
Domestic Goddess on a Budget

Some of the material in this book has been published before in columns in the *Herald on Sunday*, *New Zealand Women's Weekly* and *NZ Gardener*. The publisher would like to thank them for their assistance.

Allen & Unwin
Sydney, Melbourne, Auckland, London

83 Alexander Street
Crows Nest NSW 2065
Australia
Phone: (61 2) 8425 0100
Fax: (61 2) 9906 2218
Email: info@allenandunwin.com
Web: www.allenandunwin.com

National Library of New Zealand Cataloguing-in-Publication Data

Nissen, Wendyl.
A home companion : my year of living like my grandmother / Wendyl
Nissen. 2nd ed.
Previous ed.: Crows Nest, NSW, 2010.
Includes bibliographical references and index.
ISBN 978-1-877505-14-0
1. Nissen, Wendyl. 2. Home economics. 3. Self-reliant living—New Zealand.
4. Sustainable living—New Zealand.
640—dc 22

ISBN 978 1 877505 14 0

Set in 11pt Mrs Eaves by Katy Yiakmis
Internal design and illustrations by Katy Yiakmis
Printed in Australia by McPherson's Printing Group

10 9 8 7 6 5 4 3 2 1

This book is dedicated to my three nanas:
Olive Peterson
Eileen Letica
Marguerite Nissen

Introduction

I clip our granddaughter Lila into her car seat and give her a kiss. I lean into the car and kiss my 12-year-old daughter Pearl and husband Paul before waving them off. As I turn to walk back to my caravan I feel the most overwhelming sense of freedom. Just me. Alone. For three days. Bliss.

I hastily tidy up after a weekend of sun and sand, endless reading of books to Lila, helping Pearl sort everything out for school camp the following week, glasses of wine shared with Paul as we watch the sun go down, exhausted as our middle-aged bodies adjust to running around after a toddler. I pull out the old Formica table, place my old laptop on it, reach for my favourite pillow to put behind my back and fire up the computer.

As I wait for it to clunk into life I look out at my view. Crystal blue water at high tide laps just metres away, a taupe coloured sandbank breaks the horizon and then there is more blue behind it. Crisp lines of surf, rolling in endlessly. Local kids play in the water practising swear words on each other, a German tourist fishes hopefully and my dog Shirl is under the table, head resting on my feet as she lets out a contented sigh.

I am about to start the fourth book I have written at this table, in this caravan, looking at this view and a sense of complete calm comes over me.

What I write will be part journal, part instruction manual for any woman who finds herself yearning to get her hands covered in soil, rid her house of toxic chemicals, nurture her family and become a green goddess. Even if it's just at the weekends.

What qualifies me to write this book is that in the past six years I have made the transition from a high-flying corporate animal to a green goddess nana. Some of you may have read my book *Bitch and Famous* which details the years I spent as a hard-bitten journalist then editor of several women's magazines. I was a take-no-prisoners sort of girl and like many in my generation was determined to craft a successful career no matter how many hours I had to work and how many enemies I had to make.

Then I just stopped. I reassessed the things that were important in my life and it came down to a select group of people – my family. You can have all the money in the world, all the success you want, all the fame and all the friends but without a happy family I believe you are deprived of one of the most basic joys in life.

So I came home to work and discovered the ancient art of nurturing and somewhere along the way harnessed a goddess or two I found lurking within. I wrote the book *Domestic Goddess on a Budget* as a result of five years in my home exploring safer, less toxic ways of living. In it I shared over

100 natural recipes for beauty and cleaning that I had found by wading through old recipe books that I'd found in op shops, looking for old-fashioned alternatives. It sold well and developed a large following, thousands of whom I email with a newsletter every Thursday afternoon. It seemed natural to follow up that book with a home journal. It started off as 'how I became a mad hippy in one far out year' and finished up as simply *A Home Companion*.

In it, you will find some old favourite recipes and a lot of new ones. You will also find a month by month seasonal analysis of the discoveries I have made throughout the year. In a way the research process has been very similar to *Domestic Goddess on a Budget* where I sat down and trawled old books to find recipes, tested them out, adjusted them and then shared. But my research for this book has also involved trawling through the 168 columns and the 52 email newsletters I write in a year. I also dug out many books and read them again, pulling out the salient points I had taken from them. Then I needed to grab my recipe books and my notebook where I write down every precious new recipe as I test it — from making perfume to baby wipes and blueing powder to make those sheets whiter than white!

Every recipe in this book has been tested by me and will work, I guarantee it (as long as you follow my directions). Too often the recipes you can find on the internet or in the old and new books just don't work and need substantial adjustment. It may be that the ingredients Nana used are different now, the recipe is American where raw products are different or — as I think happens a lot with recipes — someone just wrote one up and never actually tested it. Testing is half the fun for me and few visitors to my house get away without clutching a pot of something I need them to use for a week and then report back to me on.

I want this book to change the way people think about the world we live in, while still being reasonably entertaining! We need to remember that before the early 1900s we all ate organic food. The chemicals we live with every day in our food, our cleaning products, our beauty products and our work environments have only been around for about 90 years. And as a result we are suffering the consequences with a global water shortage, toxic waste dumps, global warming and shocking rises in the rates of asthma, diabetes, obesity and cancer.

I believe it's time to stop and return to the life our nana or our great nana lived while we can still remember how they lived. The only investment you need to make is your time — time to find the ingredients, time to make up the recipes, dig a garden, wait for bread to rise. All things you can do in the hours you might otherwise spend watching television at night.

My hope is that this book will end up on the bookshelf in your kitchen, just like the old scrapbook Nana used to have filled with recipes, tips and hints given to her by friends or clipped out of a newspaper or magazine. And just like Nana's scrapbook I hope it becomes stained with use, a chocolate-icing stain here, a smudge of oil there and a dusting of baking soda stuck in the spine. I hope you use it well and use it often and add to it with your own notes, clippings and recipes. And when you get old and become a nana yourself, I hope that you pass it on to someone you love so that they too, can live a healthy, chemical-free existence.

OCTOBER

he first week of October is always a busy one in our house. We have daughter Alex's birthday on the second, my father Cedric's birthday on the third and our wedding anniversary on the fourth. Some years our kitchen has churned out three celebration meals in a row. Once that week is over I always turn myself over to spring because it is the perfect time to embark on change. There's a reason Nana used to spring clean at this time of year — dragging blankets out to air, washing and drying curtains in the sun with the first real heat we've seen for months. Dusting, mopping and getting everything shipshape was vital for a good old clean-up. Thankfully, these days we don't cart all the furniture outside and whitewash the walls or beat the carpets out on the lawn or scrub the wooden floors.

One of my gorgeous old books *Household Discoveries* advised the housewife to arrange for spring cleaning by preparing food such as ham and pies in advance, dressing appropriately in bloomers made of four widths of heavy dark skirting and making a lotion out of quince seed, glycerine, borax and witch-hazel for the chapped hands that would certainly result from all that cleaning. These days we might put a bit of extra effort in, but certainly not to the extent of stocking up on food and wearing bloomers!

I always notice the windows in October as the sun shines through and reveals all the grime from winter and so out comes my vinegar-based glass cleaner. Only as the light improves do I notice the dust marks which have lurked in the grim light of winter so I make a huge batch of lemon dusters and get wiping. But October also gets to work on a more emotional, spiritual level as it reawakens me after the cold, grey winter when I've barely left the comfort of my goosedown puffer jacket. I love the feel of the sun's warmth on my skin and can't help but feel rejuvenated.

I notice that almost overnight the garden has sprung into life. Weeds which have lain dormant over the winter pop their heads up. My tomato seedlings, which have grudgingly sprouted but done little else, suddenly take off and I am always overtaken with a flurry of activity getting the garden planted and ready for the summer season.

I wanted to begin this book with the month of October because during the past six years two events happened in October that helped propel me towards my green goddess nana lifestyle.

The first was buying our old blue and white 1968 Lightweight caravan in October 2005. My father and I picked her up from a farm in Kawhia where she had been used to house shearers. We then tentatively towed her across the North Island to her new home by the beach at the camping ground.

When we got there Dad took a good look at her axles and breathed a sigh of relief.

'Lucky we made it,' he said. 'Should have bought a brand new one.'

Dad and I have differing views when it comes to old things. The ultimate Kiwi DIY bloke he has spent his life fixing up houses, cars, baches and appliances and now he likes things to be new, new, new. Sparkling new.

When we bought our old villa in Grey Lynn he shook his head in dismay and he thought my old caravan was a bad investment too. I try to explain to him that I like old things, that our villa and our caravan were built to last. They might be a bit tatty around the edges but our house is made from heart kauri and has lasted for more than 100 years so far. It also breathes – no condensation or leaky buildings for us. And as long as no developers pull it down, it will easily stand for another 100 years. As for the caravan, it's solid sheet metal. With no insulation, it's bloody freezing in the winter but in a storm it hunkers down like a Waiouru army tank and does battle with the elements.

Initially the caravan was just for me. My husband, Paul, had never camped as a child and didn't really get the concept but he accepted that as part of my letting go of corporate life, I needed some time alone, preferably at a beach. Like most Kiwis I find the beach remarkably healing and I can sit and stare at the waves and changing tides for hours on end.

I believe that all women need some time alone at various stages in their lives. Anyone born after the 1960s was told that girls can do anything so we ended up doing everything. If you're anything like me, eventually you reach a point where nothing seems to happen in your family's lives without you. Finding the peanut butter, taking the dog to the vet, nursing children through sickness, sadness and stress, supporting our partners through sickness, sadness and stress, going out to work, cooking nutritionally balanced and eco-friendly meals until one day you just stop. Because you are unable to answer the question: 'What about me?'

I needed to stop being everything to everyone. I needed to be everything for me before I could be there for others. Just like the oxygen mask which pops down in front of you during an emergency on an aeroplane, you need to take the oxygen first before you can help your child.

When I talk to women's groups I encourage them to go home and find a picture of themselves when they were 20. They all go quiet and get a funny look on their face. They are remembering that vibrant young thing who had hopes and dreams, and somewhere along the way many of those hopes and dreams flew out the window never to be seen again. I encourage them to reignite a few of their dreams, from just getting on a surfboard again to booking a plane ticket to Europe.

When I bought the caravan I miraculously found the energy of my inner 20-year-old and spent a few days ripping up the old carpet and revealing gorgeous gold-flecked Formica. I found a great old recipe for a lino polish, which I mixed and rubbed on with love. I washed down the ceiling to reveal a stunning gold sparkly and it got a rub of lino polish as well. I sewed fresh, crisp cream cotton curtains on my old Singer sewing machine (which I have had since I was 20) and bought the best linens and tableware for my sanctuary. And then I popped down there every so often just to be with me and find out what the hell I wanted out of life.

I was lucky that my children, and most importantly my husband, understood about this sudden urge. Paul would hold the fort making sure the kids got to school and were looked after while I sat and gazed at the sea. For some women,

I understand that getting away is not that easy. They are concerned that while they are away the whole world will come to a stop, their children will starve and their husband will forget to get the kids to school.

If you're one of those women, to you I say try it. Just for one or two nights. You might return to a messy house and a few slightly more dishevelled members of your family than usual but they will have found the cereal and heated up baked beans and survived. You might just be surprised at how good you feel when you walk back in that door. Refreshed, revived, re-energised with a stronger sense of self than you have had in years.

Some women just don't have husbands who can cope without them. If that's you then I have to point out it's your fault for letting that happen. Any man can make toast, get children dressed and drive them to school. The fact that yours can't do these things means that he has never had to. For you, I'm going to suggest the same prescription. Just go. He'll cope. Leave lists and turn your phone off.

I have a routine that I follow when I get to the caravan. I clear it out, dust around for spiders, make up the bed with my crisp, white linen and then walk over to my friend Maria's caravan where she has a fragrant lavender bush growing. I pick a bunch of lavender sprigs and bring them back to put in the special vase on the table. Then I lie on the bed and watch the sea.

Over the years my caravan, like any good friend, has spread its joy to the rest of my family. Paul now loves nothing better than time spent at the caravan where he cooks a mean charcoal barbecue. He will even walk on the beach barefoot – something he was unable to do previously as he didn't like the feel of the sand in his toes. Our four adult children and two nieces use the caravan frequently, especially on New Year's Eve with their many friends — we stay at home in the city for some peace and quiet. We've also had some lovely times there with good friends. And we all spend time with my parents who have a nice, new British caravan next door. They found our camping spot first and spend up to four months of the year on—and-off living there. And of course our granddaughter Lila has joined the fan club asking for 'Grandma's caravan beach' whenever she can.

I'm not suggesting all women charge off and buy an old caravan, but having a caravan attitude can do wonders for your ying and yang, your inner peace, your finding out who the hell you are after all these years. Maybe it's a night on your own in a hotel or motel — make sure it has a bath — borrow a friend's bach, or simply mind a friend's house while they are out of town. Just make sure you find the physical space you need.

On that first trip when I stripped down the caravan and brought her back to her former glory, I invented my Turkish Gin which has now become synonymous with my time alone. It tastes like a gin-soaked Turkish Delight. My friend Ian, who runs the camp, wandered up in the afternoon to see how I was getting on with my renovations and found me sitting outside in my deck chair sipping my new concoction looking blissfully happy and contented with myself.

'Drinking already?' he asked with a smile on his face.

'See all that carpet? Ripped it all out with my bare hands,' I skited.

'You deserve a drink then,' he laughed. 'Even if it is only two o'clock in the afternoon.'

What I hadn't realised during my frenzied renovations was that the caravan sits in the shadow of a hill so the light goes early in the afternoon. I had thought it was early evening!

I've never begun drinking that early at the caravan again, but I've certainly always looked forward to my Turkish Gin.

My love affair with my caravan has meant I always have somewhere to go to write my books, get other writing projects finished or just get away for a breather. I always pack nice food just for me because I don't have to cook for an army and can indulge myself in the meals I really love, which are often the healthiest ones for me.

You'll be thinking I eat fresh salads accompanied by poached white fish and cleansing mineral water. But actually what I crave to eat when I'm on my own is liver. I'll say it again . . . liver. In my opinion it is a highly under-rated health food, low in saturated fats and cholesterol and high in vitamins A, B6, B12 and D, as well as being a great source of protein. There's also iron, zinc, copper, manganese, riboflavin, thiamine, niacin, folate, pantothenic acid, phosphorus and selenium.

Research shows that — possibly as a result of our determination to beat skin cancer by keeping out of the sun — around half of New Zealand adults don't get enough vitamin D and 4 per cent of women and 2 per cent of men are vitamin D-deficient. Our main source of vitamin D is sunlight but you can also get it from foods like liver. There is growing evidence that having an adequate level of vitamin D can prevent or improve the outcome of many diseases including breast, prostate and bowel cancer, cardiovascular disease, diabetes and multiple sclerosis. There is even a possible association between low levels and obesity. So liver is more than a health food, it's a bloody tonic!

After a long winter I often feel a bit rundown so a course of liver once a week — yes, just like Nana used to eat — is a great pick-me-up. In May, when tamarillos are in season I throw them in with the liver, fried onions and some of my homemade Worcestershire sauce and am immediately transported to my happy place.

Eating liver also honours the killing of animals by eating every part of its body and not wasting anything. There's a reason wild beasts like lions go straight for the liver when they've killed an antelope — it's the most nutritious part of the animal. My caravan and I have shared many happy liver nights together far away from the 'yucks' and 'ew, how can you?' reactions I get at home.

The other October event that changed my life was picking up our three hens Marigold, Yoko and Hillary. I had wanted chickens for a couple of years but after researching poultry-keeping I was put off by disturbing stories of eggs getting stuck in hen's bottoms, prolapsed uteruses, and other nasty diseases. Then, one day we were at the caravan and I'd been talking to the camp owners about their hens, which roam freely around the place and represent just about every poultry breed I've ever seen. They had just produced a batch of chicks which got me thinking and I said to Paul, 'Imagine making our own food and knowing what went into it from the beginning and eating something entirely created on our own property?'

'We already do that,' he replied. 'We have an organic garden.'

'Yes but what if we could create our own protein, keep our own hens? Everyone used to do it in the old days. They all had a couple of hens out the back.'

'No,' was all he said.

Half an hour later I used my latest weapon for getting what I want.

'Lila would love them.'

'She would, wouldn't she?' he smiled, thinking about his

baby granddaughter growing up and chasing hens around the yard, like something out of *The Darling Buds of May*.

'I'll just look into it,' I nudged.

'Mmm, okay, just look into it.'

Two weeks later the hen house arrived, beautifully made by a man I found on TradeMe.

Two weeks after that we picked up our pullets from a lovely woman in South Auckland who had hand reared them. They were very tame, which was great — as a first time hen keeper I wanted to make sure I could catch them easily.

We named them in the car on the way home each getting to name one hen. Pearl immediately chose Yoko, enjoying her wit and humour all the way home. I chose Marigold because it seemed like an old-fashioned name my nana might have used for her hen. Paul chose Hillary, after Hillary Clinton, enjoying his wit and humour all the way home.

'They're all yours,' announced Paul when I released them from their cages. 'I'm having nothing to do with them.'

I proceeded to fall in love with them from the moment I got them home. It wasn't long before I was suffering from hentionitis, as it became known in our household. It's related to 'mentionitis' the disease that inflicts a woman who finds a man so fascinating that she insists on mentioning him in every sentence, much to the irritation of her husband.

I found myself wandering out to the garden to watch them. A habit I still find more soothing than the deepest meditation. It also helps you realise the true meaning of the commonly used phrases: 'hen pecked' 'pecking order' and 'hen party'. As I watch them scratch the ground, peck about and generally have a very busy day raiding the garden for snails, slugs and green edibles I marvel at their natural instinct and how that is denied them in battery farms.

Initially self-sufficiency plans didn't quite come to

fruition because of my insistence on feeding them only organic feed, creating a unique blend which cost the equivalent of Angus steak all round for a week. Then there were the frequent hand-fed treats of grapes, sultanas and corn.

Once they were 20 weeks old, which was time to start laying, they seemed to show no indication of producing protein, preferring to chase each other around the garden and feast on the range of herbs and greens I had grown especially for them.

'When these eggs finally arrive they'll work out at $17 each,' grumped my husband as he gently stroked Hillary's neck.

For a man determined to have nothing to do with the chickens he was showing a lot of affection towards them and I'd often find him out the back chatting with Marigold, Yoko and Hillary.

'No I wasn't,' he'd say. 'I thought there was a lost child stuck in the tree.'

He's still the first out in the morning to let the cackling gaggle of hens — who at that time are pressed against the henhouse door, doing a very good impression of ladies waiting for the Smith and Caughey sale to open — out of their coop.

And he's the last one out to have a chat and close them up safely for the night in their coop.

By the end of October we knew that eventually, of course, they would have to start laying. But what we didn't know was that within months I would be thinking dark thoughts about wringing their necks.

Lemon Dusters

½ cup water

½ cup white vinegar

3–4 lemons

6 drops lemon essential oil

6 to 8 dusters (made from old towels, cloth nappies or sheets)

Mix equal quantities of water and white vinegar in a bowl. Add lemon essential oil. Soak your clean dusters in the bowl and squeeze liquid out so that they are damp. Peel the rind off the lemons and lay a couple of pieces on each cloth. Roll up cloths lengthwise, and then roll the other way into a ball. Place these one on top of each other in a jar, throw in the occasional extra piece of rind and screw on the lid. Take the dusters out when you need to use them. If they aren't too soiled you can roll them back up and use them again. The smell in the room is divine.

Lino Polish

1 cup white vinegar

1 cup turpentine

½ cup raw linseed oil

Mix all the ingredients in a glass bottle or jar. Shake well. Rub the mixture onto the lino with a cloth, then polish with another clean cloth. Shake bottle frequently.

Rose Syrup

400 grams sugar

250 ml water

1 tablespoon lemon juice

75 ml rosewater

a few drops of grenadine for colour

Put the sugar and water in a pan and heat gently, stirring occasionally until the sugar is dissolved. Add the lemon juice and simmer for 10 minutes – do not stir. Add the rosewater and grenadine. Stir and simmer until it thickens slightly – a few minutes. Remove from the heat and let cool before pouring into clean bottles and store in the fridge.

Turkish Gin

To make the Turkish Gin, fill a tall glass with ice. Pour over 1 tablespoon of rose syrup. If you don't feel like making the syrup, it is available in many Asian and Indian food shops. Add the juice of half a lemon, a shot of gin and top up with soda water. Stir vigorously until all the rose syrup is dissolved and the drink is an intoxicating pink colour. Sit back, look at the view and enjoy.

If you're not a gin fan, this works equally well with vodka.

Gorgeous Liver

Take 200 grams of liver and slice it to create ⸤
of meat about 10mm thick, removing any sinew
tissue. Roughly chop the flesh of two tamarillos and
mix with the liver in a bowl. Leave to marinate for 10
minutes. Finely slice an onion and fry it gently in a
little olive oil over a medium heat. When the onion is
just starting to brown, turn up the heat a little and add
the liver and tamarillos. Fry the liver quickly on one
side for a minute and then flip it over to brown the
other side. Just as it has finished cooking swish in about
a tablespoon of Worcestershire sauce and let it bubble
and caramelise down into the pan, which should only
take a second. Swish it all around so that the meat is
coated with the tamarillo and the sauce and serve.

Liver Casserole

I was inspired to make this when I tinkered with a very
basic recipe for Scottish Liver Pie I found in an old
Aunt Daisy cookbook and it is delicious!

Slice liver in thin pieces, roll in seasoned flour,
and lay it in a casserole dish. Add a rasher of chopped
bacon to the liver. Pour over about 2 tablespoons of
Worcestershire sauce. Cover with a layer of tomatoes,
then a layer of chopped fried onions and finally a layer
of thinly sliced raw potatoes. Add dabs of duck fat or
the fat saved from cooking bacon. Put on the lid and
bake slowly at 150°C for an hour. When cooked take off
lid and allow the potatoes to brown on the top, then
serve.

Milk Bath
(for quiet nights alone)

Using this soak results in wonderfully smooth, silky skin. The lactic acid in milk dissolves dead skin cells, the honey moisturises your skin and acts as an anti-bacterial agent and the lavender oil just relaxes you into a heavenly state.

3 cups full-fat milk powder (no place for skim milk here)

½ cup runny honey

10 drops lavender essential oil

Put all the ingredients in your hot bath as it is running, light a candle and soak away.

Quick and Easy Make-up Remover

There's no excuse for smudged mascara even when you are hiding from the world, especially if there's a potato to hand. Peel the potato first – or you'll get mud in your eyes – then slice it thinly. Use the potato slice to wipe away your eye makeup. Wipe off excess potato juice with a tissue. You'll be amazed at how good this is.

A QUICK GUIDE TO KEEPING HENS

The Henhouse

In this country we don't have to worry about foxes taking our chickens at night so for free-range hens, a henhouse is really just somewhere out of the rain and wind where they can sleep and lay eggs. Even when they have a henhouse, they will usually end up making a nest somewhere in the garden where they prefer to lay.

There are many henhouse designs available on the internet. Whatever you choose, you need to make sure it has perches up high as hens like to sleep roosting on these. Some henhouses have a little door at the back which opens into the nest boxes for easy egg collection. Ours just has two boxes that are easily reached from the door.

Make sure it has adequate ventilation and no drafts as chickens hate the damp.

It is also important that the henhouse is easy to clean out. I give my henhouse a good squirt with the hose once a week, then change the hay in the nest boxes and pick up any droppings off the floor. Once you have done all this spray the whole place with neat white vinegar to kill any lingering germs.

Your hens will put themselves to bed at night because they are really blind in the dark and need to know they will be safe. All you need to remember is to shut the door to the henhouse before you go to bed in case some rabid tomcat decides to have a go at the hens in the night.

Choosing your hens

If this is your first adventure with hens I strongly advise that you get them from someone who has hand-raised them so that they are reasonably tame. Good breeds to choose for egg production are Red or Brown Shavers. As pullets – hens aged around 20 weeks – they will still be quite light on their feet so expect them to fly quite high, until they put on weight and can only leap a bit. Your hens should start laying any time after 20 weeks old.

Other pets

Hens can hold their own against cats and most dogs will leave them alone but if you're worried you can fence the hens in. Our dog is actually quite frightened of them. But there are some breeds of dogs that just can't leave a hen alone so check that out with your vet before you bring hens home.

Urban restrictions

Most city councils will have a ruling on how many hens you can keep on your property and most will not allow roosters. The council where I live allows six hens. It is important to have more than one as they like to be part of a social group – three is the best number to start with.

Some people are confused about the role of the rooster. You only need one if you want to breed your birds, otherwise hens will happily ovulate (make an egg) every day without a rooster around to fertilise them.

Food

You can buy commercial chicken feed at most supermarkets, although I prefer to buy mine from a supplier who opts out of using meat by-products. The good thing about a commercial laying formula is that you can be sure the hens are getting all the nutrition they need. However if you plan to free-range your birds and feed them kitchen scraps they will get plenty of everything they need from your leftovers as well as slugs, insects and garden weeds.

You can make your own feed using my recipe if you want to spoil them (see page 28).

The hens will also need a supply of grit to keep in their crop where they grind up grains and grasses and supply calcium for egg shell production. Fresh, clean water replaced daily is important too. Hens drink a lot of water in hot weather, so do keep an eye on it.

I also give mine regular feeds of milk products like the whey from my cheese making, or yoghurt and cottage cheese to ensure they get enough calcium.

Incredibly Expensive Hen Food

Where possible, I buy organic produce for this recipe.

1 kg jumbo oats

1 kg rye

1 kg bran

1 kg wheat

1 kg brown rice

1 kg sunflower seeds

250 grams linseed

250 grams sea kelp granules

500 grams brewer's yeast

Mix together and serve three very happy hens.

One hen will need about 100 grams a day, but I just keep a feeder full and let the hens feed when they need it, which tends to be at both ends of the day and a couple of times during the day.

To make it go further you can combine this half-and-half with commercial feed. You won't get purely organic eggs, but you will have very strong and healthy hens.

Leftovers

Our hens will eat everything from leftover cereal and toast, to salads and stale cake. The only thing they won't eat is citrus fruit. Don't feed green potato peel, dried beans or avocado skins as they contain toxins. Too much sugar or salt is bad for them too.

Additives

Feed your hens linseed as this supplies fibre and omega-3, which means your eggs will be even more nutritious. Alfalfa sprouts and corn will both give their eggs deep yellow yolks.

Treats

When you first get your hens, encourage them to eat treats from your hand so that they get used to you. This way they will always come when you call them and they can easily be led away from the vege patch they have invaded.

Our hens' top treats in order of preference are sultanas, grapes, corn, silverbeet and bugs from the garden.

Tonics

Add a clove of garlic and a teaspoon of cider vinegar to their water bowl. This will boost their immune systems and help their digestive systems.

Also add a teaspoon of colloidal silver, which is a liquid suspension of microscopic silver particles and is well known in alternative medicine as an antiseptic and disinfectant.

Cuddles

Hens enjoy a cuddle and as they get older, they will crouch
down on the ground to make it easier for you to pick them
up. Hens are very reactive to anything that drops a shadow on
them for two reasons. The first is as an instinctive reaction
to a rooster that might loom over them to initiate sex. The
second reason is in case of attack by a predator such as a hawk.
Because we are dominant, when we cause a shadow over them,
they crouch down obediently.

Pick them up so that you are holding their wings tightly
against their body on both sides or else they will squawk and
flap all over the place. Pull them into your side and hold them
reasonably tightly. They love to be stroked around their head
and neck very gently. And if you need to calm a hen just tip
them upside down. I'm not sure why this works but they go
very quiet!

In the Garden

If you haven't grown your own tomato seedlings, get down to the garden centre and buy some. Tomatoes traditionally go into the ground on Labour Weekend and you'll want to get some basil to plant around it as they make perfect companions in the soil as well as on your plate.

My best tip for planting tomatoes is to add a tablespoon of milk powder and a little potash to the soil under each tomato plant when planting — it seems to improve the flavour and the plants get off to a good start.

Try to use the seeds from last years' crop (see page 130 for how to do this) as your plants will already have the genetic code to survive in your garden, passed down from the parent plants. I notice that plants I buy from garden centres often come down with early blight, whereas my plants seem to withstand it.

A great tip for transplanting any seedlings or cuttings is to add one drop of Rescue Remedy per litre of water in their first watering. Rescue Remedy is a homeopathic formula made out of bach flowers, which many people use after an operation, a shock, a bump on the head or just to calm themselves during a stressful time.

NOVEMBER

One of the skills I have had to learn since moving home, far away from the corporate world, is that of patience. As a magazine editor I was not renowned for my ability to wait and see. It was now or nothing, my way or the highway, just do it and talk about it later, a good meeting is a short meeting and give it to me yesterday. If I was negotiating an exclusive story deal with a celebrity or a newsmaker and they asked for some time to think about it I'd say: 'Sure, take all the time you need, I'll ring you back in 10 minutes.' If I had asked one of my writers to chase up a story that morning and by the end of the day they hadn't got it, I would wish them a good night at home . . . on the phone. 'You'll have that story by the morning, won't you?' I would smile, ever the velvet steamroller.

These days my bread is not going to rise any quicker just because I want it to and it won't respond to threats – although it does like a hot-water bottle placed under the bowl in winter. Making a batch of laundry liquid does take – and will always take – half an hour no matter how quickly I grate and stir and pour. But it always puts me in a good mood while I'm making it thanks to the lavender oil I use in it, which has the bonus of making my kitchen smell wonderful. And my hens, Marigold, Hillary and Yoko were not going to start laying eggs, just because they were over 20 weeks old and all the books said they should. Or because I spent more time than I should creeping up on them in the bushes hoping to catch them in the act. Or because I had deposited two 'pretend' plastic eggs in their nesting boxes hoping to fool them into laying an identical real one.

'I saw one of them rolling around looking like she might be in the hen equivalent of labour,' I informed my husband.

'I think that's what's called having a dust bath,' he pointed out.

'Do you think I should play them a rooster call to stir them into action?' I suggested after returning from the nest box empty. The hens were now officially 22 weeks old.

'Where would you get that from?' he asked reasonably.

'I think my cell phone has one as a ringtone,' I said, impatiently pushing buttons and finding only a salsa tune.

In the end I had to simply accept that my hens were more interested in expending energy on escaping my carefully erected chicken-wire fences, than settling into the nesting box producing eggs.

I simply had to find other things to do while I waited, like getting my picking garden in order. The wonderful thing about warmer weather is that salad greens start growing so quickly that if you have a good bed full you can take a leaf or two from each plant for a fresh, nutritious salad at lunchtime and dinnertime and the next day they seem to have miraculously been replaced. The plants can go on like this for months before they bolt to seed in the hot weeks of January.

In Auckland we can grow salad, especially cos lettuce and rocket, right through winter but it is slow going.

While I kept an eye on my hens for imminent egg arrival, I planted out a garden bed with a dozen plants of cos and oak leaf lettuce I had bought from the garden centre. Then I liberally sprinkled around rocket and endive seeds, which always pop up within a few days in warm weather as long as you keep them moist.

These can all be picked one or two leaves at a time from the outside of the plant by using your thumbnail and just nipping the leaf at the base. This way you don't harm the plant and it will generously grow more leaves for you.

I bring the leaves in and simply put them in the sink and fill it with water. I leave them to soak while I do something else for dinner and when I come back any dirt or bugs have simply sunk to the bottom of the sink. I whip the leaves out, throw them in the salad spinner, add my simple sesame-lemon dressing and there is our salad, positively heaving with goodness.

There are so many advantages to picking vegetables just before you are about to eat them. There is the flavour which is so fresh and crisp — nothing like the limp offerings you buy pre-washed and prepared in bags at the supermarket. There is also the fact that you know what has been sprayed on them, used to fertilise them and what they have been rinsed in, which in our case is absolutely nothing. The salad you buy in those bags will often have been fertilised with chemicals, or sprayed with chemical pesticides and some are even soaked in chemicals before they are bagged in gas to make them last longer.

Then there is the fact that the minute a vegetable is harvested it starts losing some of its nutrients and vitality. Fruit and vegetables that are transported to supermarkets around the country are usually picked before they are ripe, which gives them less time to develop vitamins and minerals. They may look ripe but they will never have the same nutritional value as they would have had they been allowed to ripen naturally. They are also exposed to heat and light, which degrades some nutrients.

I recently saw boxes of 'fresh' veges sitting outside my local supermarket in the sun, waiting to be taken inside. You can only wonder what condition they were in by the time they reached the cooling sprays in the vegetable aisle. Picking a fully mature vegetable or fruit as close as you can to eating it has to be the best use of your garden. Sometimes I grow iceberg because it is my favourite lettuce and Pearl loves it too. There is nothing better than a fresh crisp iceberg leaf thrown in the mouth and crunched to your heart's content. Occasionally Pearl and I sit with an iceberg chopped up and dip the leaves in our favourite feta and spinach dip. But when you grow them you do have to leave them until they are fully formed and I lack the . . . there's that word again . . . patience.

The closer I get to nature and self sufficiency the more I realise that being patient is not a waste of time where you hang around and nothing gets achieved, which is how I used to view it in my former high-stress life. Now when something doesn't happen when I think it should, I see it as an opportunity to do something else while I wait.

This is when my attention often turns to sheets. White sheets — or sheets that should be whiter. One of the things I loved about Paul when I first met him was that he was a crisp, white-sheet man. Paul had a one hundred per cent cotton, gorgeous weave, beautifully-made bed complete with hospital corners, unlike most of the men I knew who still slept between the polycotton print sheets their mums had given them when they went flatting and whose idea of clean sheets meant you washed them once a month. My love affair with white sheets – and Paul – has meant a desire to keep the sheets crisp and white, which gets difficult after a while. Constant washing with commercial laundry detergents leaves white sheets clean but with a grey/yellow tinge to them that no amount of soaking or bleaching can get rid of. There's a reason for this.

Commercial laundry powders and liquids have been developed to leave a residue in your clothes and linen, which they call optical brighteners or whiteners. These attach to fabric and when hit by ultraviolet light they change the light's wavelengths coming off the clothes. The optical whiteners stay in your clothes, are absorbed through your skin and can affect your immune system. They are thought to cause allergic skin reactions in babies and children. What they also tend to do is leave our white sheets grubby. And just in case you didn't know, most commercial laundry detergents consist largely of washing soda with variations in the types of artificial fragrance, colour and additives mixed in.

I remember my nana used a product called Blue, made by Reckitt's. The label on it was a beautifully designed piece of Kiwiana with the catchphrases 'Clothes always snowy' and 'Clothes always fresh'. The Blue came in a little netting bag and you threw it in your washing during your final rinse. It could also be used to treat bee stings and insect bites. You could even clean windows with it.

The blue pigment corrects the yellow/grey pigment and returns the material to 'brighter than white!'

You can't buy Blue here any longer, although you can still get it in Australia, so I set about creating my own Blue

36

equivalent. The blueing powder is created out of Prussian Blue pigment, which is the most extraordinary thing to behold. The deep blue colour is astonishing and has been used for centuries by painters. It was even once used in some armies during the Second World War to reduce sexual urges. Apparently they would slip it into the soldiers' coffee and all desire would be diminished, which I'm sure made things a lot more peaceful in the barracks.

You can buy Prussian Blue powder at art shops. We source ours directly from the USA though Paul is determined to get some from Germany so he can say we get our Prussian Blue from Prussia.

I mix the blueing powder with baking soda and then add it to the final rinse. While I was trying to get the recipe right I ruined about three sets of our beautiful, expensive white sheets which to this day have blue blotches on them. When I finally got the mix right, I then hung the sheets out in blinding sunshine to dry and Paul, who hadn't been aware I was even making the blueing powder, came in from the line holding up a sheet and saying: 'Did you bleach these, I've never seen them so white!'

I sometimes hear from people who have made or bought my blueing powder and have not waited until the washing machine bowl is completely full for the rinse cycle before adding the powder. They also end up with blotches on their sheets. I now know that you simply throw them back in, washing them as normal with warm water and my laundry liquid and the blotches will wash out. Don't let them dry as I did! By the way if you have a front loader, just put the blueing powder in the fabric softener container as I'm told this works well.

I always wait for a bright sunny day before I wash my sheets, which is why I love November when the heat of the sun returns. It's a great time to take the opportunity to go through the linen cupboard and freshen everything up.

Sunlight is a fantastic bleaching agent, it's free and it's effective. I've often hung a stained piece of clothing out disappointed that I couldn't quite get the spot out and then collected it at the end of the day only to find the mark completely gone. If the stain is harder to shift, try the lemon and sunshine stain remover recipe on page 54.

I've had hundreds of enthusiastic emails from people who tell me stories of old sheets and articles of clothing they had given up on and then managed to revitalise with a bit of blueing. And one story I wish I hadn't heard was from a woman who emailed me to say she used it on her elderly husband's undies. 'He has the occasional accident so it's nice to be able to get them white again,' she shared.

I will stress that the blueing powder is not a soaker like NapiSan or bleach. It won't get stains out, it just corrects the overall pigment. I try not to use bleach, even though Nana used heaps of it. If I need to give something a good soak I tend to use the Ecostore laundry soaker as it avoids many of the harmful chemicals associated with other soakers and works really well.

With the gentle heat of November comes a general stripping of clothes on my part. Out from under my three layers of jumpers, my puffer jacket and my jeans and ugg boots emerge arms, legs, feet and hands, wrinkly and wizened from the drying effects of winter. I look at my pale, flaky skin and find it difficult to imagine that by February it will be golden and gleaming, but it will, thanks to my body oil.

For many women this is the time they reach for the fake tan, or the moisturisers that promise a gradual tan. I just need one smell of the stuff to know it's not going anywhere near me. I don't put anything on my skin that I wouldn't eat for the simple reason that most of what goes on the skin ends up in the bloodstream due to the permeable nature of our body's largest organ. Applying the 'would I eat that?' test is an easy way to ensure that synthetic chemicals, possibly tested on animals, and made out of God only knows what will not be shot into my bloodstream because someone on a TV commercial tells me that I'm worth it.

None of us truly believe that a celebrity advertising a certain beauty cream actually looks that way because of the cream. Suzanne Somers takes 60 pills and submits to several injections a day to keep herself beautiful. Kate Moss zaps herself with micro-electric currents, Jessica Simpson reportedly spends $25,000 a pop on beauty preparations just to get camera ready and apparently Nicolette Sheridan is addicted to her La Prairie cream at $1000 a jar. Then there are the Botox injections and the cosmetic surgery. I don't want to look like any of these women, do you?

I recently read a survey which found that the average British woman hosts 515 chemicals on her body every day once she has applied deodorant, body and facial moisturiser, and make-up. And if those *Coro St* actresses are anything to go by, at least another hundred chemicals in the fake tan!

I think studies like this need to be read with some caution as they are usually funded by a corporation eager to sell their own products, in this case a deodorant maker. But it is interesting that beauty products in this country are self regulated, which means the manufacturers can put anything they like in them, unlike food manufacturers who must submit to rigorous testing and regulations.

The beauty product manufacturers might list their ingredients on the labels or they might not. But any locally-made product that is exported must comply with other countries' much stricter regulations that require full disclosure of all ingredients. If you do find an ingredient listed they might hide it under a chemical name you won't understand. I have become accustomed to cosmetic companies liberally throwing herbs and nuts around on their packaging with words like 'botanicals' and 'marine' to give the impression they are a natural product despite listing in their ingredients methyl, propyl, butyl and ethyl paraben, toxic mineral and petroleum oils, the controversial and potentially carcinogenic sodium laurel sulphate and a bit of a synthetic fragrance and artificial colouring to top it all off.

I'm more than happy to spend the same amount of money – but usually a lot less – than I would on a L'Oréal, Clarins, Lancôme or Chanel on a Weleda, Living Nature or Dr Hauschka product because I can understand what is on their labels, and I know that as exporters they have complied with EU standards and have given full disclosure of their ingredients.

It has only been in the past few decades that governments and regulation officials have come to realise that our skin absorbs everything we put on it. Prior to that, it was widely believed that our skin was waterproof, like a raincoat, so there was no need to worry about what was in beauty products.

The biggest issue for 'natural' cosmetic manufacturers is preserving their products so that they can be transported around the world and then sit on shelves for up to two years – cosmetics which use synthetic ingredients last for years. Finding a natural preservative is very hard because something which is completely natural will always have a lifespan, just like yoghurt or bread.

Living Nature, which operates out of Kerikeri, in Northland, has managed to harness the preservative qualities of manuka oil blended with other ingredients. That meant that some of their early formulations smelt strongly of manuka oil which wasn't great, but they have recently reformulated their products to smell a lot more feminine. I use the Living Nature nourishing night cream with a few drops of their radiance night oil mixed in and go to bed smelling like a gorgeous red rose.

I spent a few days with Living Nature to try to understand how you can make natural cosmetics without resorting to synthetics and was really impressed with the effort that the company puts into ensuring their products stand up to the highest scrutiny. They use native plants from the bush for many of their formulations as well as white clay from a nearby mine and honey from local hives. Their bottles are made out of a special plastic to lessen environmental impact and all of their packaging is recyclable.

I love a good red lipstick – but a recent study found that two companies, L'Oréal and Cover Girl, had levels of lead in their red lipsticks exposing women to the harmful neurotoxin. The EU bans lead in all lipsticks. Yet here they aren't required to list it on the ingredients and the two manufacturers concerned claimed that there were only trace amounts included and that they believed there was no health risk to consumers. Most disturbingly the only action taken for New Zealand women was advice from the National Poison Centre suggesting that as lead poisoning occurs over time, the only way to know how much harm regular small doses of lead causes is to get a blood test! Which hammers home the message that when it comes to caring for our health, we need to do it ourselves and not wait for a law change or even a ban by our government to protect us. These cosmetic companies use lead oxide to get the red colour in their lipsticks but some natural cosmetic companies like Living Nature use cochineal or carmine, which our nanas probably used, but it is extracted

41

from the insect of the same name. So we might not be getting poisoned by lead but now we are squashing insects for beauty.

You might be surprised how many supposedly natural products are still using synthetic preservatives and you have a right to ring the manufacturers up and ask them why. Parabens are a concern because some studies have found that they may mimic the hormone oestrogen, which is known to play a role in breast cancer. You will find all sorts of conflicting evidence on the internet, but I prefer to opt out while there are multinational cosmetic companies keen to create confusion. The irony is some 'natural' cosmetic producers have taken out synthetic parabens which is great but they've simply replaced them with another synthetic preservative, most commonly phenoxyethanol, which is listed by the EU as harmful and an irritant. A good test to see if your product contains natural ingredients is to take some of the product you are using and expose it to light and air on a windowsill. See what happens to it. If it is a natural product it will grow mould or start to break down in some way. I did this with my favourite Weleda rose and calendula moisturiser and within a few weeks it was growing a healthy film of mould.

As I was doing the final edit of this book I noticed more stories appearing in the media about dangerous cosmetic ingredients particularly the use of fullerenes or nanoparticles in products that are on sale here, but have been removed from shelves in Europe and Australia.

Fullerenes are found mainly in anti-ageing creams, but also in hair products and face masks and are tiny ingredients there to make the products stronger and more resistant to bacteria. They are also highly toxic. Australian research has indicated that they could deeply penetrate into the skin, possibly staying in the body for as long as 40 days, posing a health risk.

In New Zealand the cosmetics industry is required by law to declare to our Environmental Risk Management Authority any use or importing of these products. There had been no reports. New Zealand is now considering legislation to bring us in line with Australia, which has begun risk assessment on nanoparticles such as fullerenes. Again, I believe your best choice is to opt out.

It is very easy to make your own beauty products, especially moisturisers and body oils, but do be aware that you need to keep them in the fridge and out of the light so that they don't go rancid. I regularly use my Magic Night Cream if my skin is especially dry and in summer I always carry around a bottle of my body oil. I rub this on day and night and my skin just soaks it up. And if I had to, I could eat it!

Another problem for cosmetics is the fragrance they add. It is rarely natural and most likely a synthetic copy of a natural smell, such as rose. Rose oil is very expensive and is the most commonly used scent in perfumes and cosmetics. It takes 2000 flowers to get a single gram of pure rose oil so you can see why it is cheaper and easier to make a synthetic chemical rose scent in a laboratory.

One way to check the toxic status of products you use is to type them into the website www.cosmeticsdatabase.com. They rate the toxicity of products on a scale of one to ten. They are very rigid in their rating systems and regard some essential oils as being toxic because they are known allergens. But if a product I like rates in the mid-range and most of that is because it contains essential oils, I am happy to use it.

The power of essential oils is well documented and they are used extensively in Indian and Chinese medicine. Way back in AD78 the Greek physician Pedanios Dioscorides published a book listing 600 medicinal plants. Many drugs we commonly use today were derived from those plants, such as morphine, which came from the poppy and was named after Morpheus the Greek god of dreams.

The perfume I use and have used since my early twenties is Chanel No 5. I love its rose/jasmine smell and it rates a massive 8 out of 10 on the cosmetic database site. Much to my horror I discovered that the only thing natural in it appears to be water.

So I have embarked on a new role as experimental perfumer, determined to replicate the world's most legendary fragrance, whose top secret formula is no doubt locked up in a bank vault somewhere in Switzerland.

Fortunately, over the years I have amassed many books on aromatherapy, and after rifling through them all I found one in which an enterprising author had made a stab at the essential oils which might be used to replicate the scent of Chanel No 5. There were nine essential oils and one powder, which was orris root. She didn't go so far as to give me a hint as to how much of each one I should use, which was completely vexing but it didn't stop me in my quest to recreate my favourite scent.

First I needed to buy the essential oils of the following: bergamot, lemon, neroli, jasmine, rose, ylang-ylang, vetiver, cedarwood and vanilla — total cost about $180.

I worked out that I could buy two bottles of Chanel No 5 for that. But then I realised that I would only need a few drops of each, so essentially I was investing in potentially bucket loads of eau de toilette.

What a lovely gift it would make, I thought to myself.

Into a glass jar I poured 70 ml of vodka and gently stirred in my oils, which I dropped in at random. I think rose got four drops, and jasmine two. The rest just went in one drop at a time. I then added a pinch of orris root, which has a lovely violet smell, and put on the lid. I left it for two days, during which time the smell seemed to change dramatically every time I sniffed it. Finally I added 30 ml of spring water and left it for another two days. Once it was ready, I filtered it through a coffee filter. I had 100 ml of eau de toilette that smelled extraordinarily gorgeous – but nothing like Chanel No 5.

'Doesn't matter,' said Pearl. 'No chemicals is what matters. Give it another name. Bouquet de Wendyl perhaps, or name it after one of the hens.'

Chanel No 5 was named by Coco Chanel because she always launched her collections on the fifth day of the fifth month and believed the number five brought her luck. This would certainly seem to be true as it is estimated that around the world a bottle of Chanel No 5 is sold every 55 seconds.

My creation simply disappears after 55 seconds and needs constant reapplication to achieve the strength of floral odour of my former perfume.

'Nothing's perfect,' said Pearl. 'At least you can be safe in the knowledge that it won't kill you.'

I now use this perfume every day, even if I do have to apply it about 20 times. As well as my No 5, I have also managed to make a very passable natural Opium-like eau de toilette.

When I'm making up recipes for cleaners I always consult my list of essential oils and their properties. It's amazing how powerful tea-tree, lavender, orange and clove oils can be at fighting bacteria while at the same time altering your mood. I've been using aromatherapy for years as an alternative to drugs when someone in my family has a cold or a headache. It's good to see more and more people catching on to how useful these oils can be in everyday life.

If you think back to Nana's era, eucalyptus oil in products like Vick's VapoRub was a common cold remedy, and they used oil of cloves for toothache. In the past decade it has become popular to use oil burners and essential oils to make a room smell nice instead of spraying around chemical-based air fresheners, which is a great step forward. But the commercial cleaning manufacturers have responded by just adding tea-tree, lavender, rose, rosemary or eucalyptus to their highly toxic mixtures.

Have a look on the label. You won't see the words 'essential oil' used anywhere. What you will see is 'fragrance' or 'perfume' because what the manufacturers have done is simply add a synthetic concoction of chemicals that matches the smell of the essential oils. These synthetic versions don't have any of the natural healing powers these oils contain. I believe part of the reason they won't use extracts of essential oils is because they would have difficulty patenting remedies that have been known for years.

This is also why you're unlikely to find your doctor recommending natural remedies, because drug companies can't make money out of a remedy you can extract yourself from a plant. Better to mix a cocktail of chemicals created in a laboratory, convince the medical profession that this is the only cure and get half the world's population reliant on them.

When I become ill I will always seek out a natural remedy if it can be found. And I am realistic that natural remedies need time to work, they won't have you up and about in three days like a strong course of antibiotics will.

A few years ago, I had a nasty breast infection which no amount of antibiotics prescribed by the breast clinic could cure. They ended up sending me away with the message that this particular infection was difficult to treat and I would just have to live with it. It wasn't life threatening or dangerous, it was just a little tender and annoying.

So I turned to natural medicines. I tried kawakawa

leaf poultices, an old Maori remedy for ulcers and sores. I tried aloe vera gel, which actually cleared it up for a little while. And finally I tried turmeric. While I was visiting my friend Paula Mason in Bali I discovered raw turmeric being sold in the markets over there as a root, similar to ginger. I read that the locals use it to heal everything. Turmeric is a natural antiseptic, preservative and anti-inflammatory. The Balinese mix it with coconut oil to treat skin diseases and fungal infections. They also drink a tonic of it called Jamu every morning. The Balinese say it helps prevent cancer, aid digestion and clears up respiratory infections.

I came home, searched high and low for the fresh root and finally found it in an Indian grocer's shop in Mt Roskill where it had been imported from Fiji. I grated it up, made a poultice and kept it plastered to my breast for a week. The infection, which I had lived with for two years, disappeared and has never returned. I now try to include turmeric in my diet every day, and if I'm feeling a bit poorly I make up a Jamu every morning until I feel better.

I thought about writing to the breast clinic to tell them of my discovery, as they had told me that other women suffer from this same infection, but I knew that they were not likely to call all their old patients in to give them some turmeric roots. I'm sure, however, that if a new antibiotic arrived care of a drug company, with a price attached, we'd all hear about it.

Please don't get me wrong, if I was seriously ill, I wouldn't be a zealot about my natural therapies. But I would combine modern drug therapy with natural therapy and give my body what I consider to be the best of both worlds.

November is always a really busy month for me as the *New Zealand Woman's Weekly* has early deadlines for columnists so that they can get their Christmas issues done ahead of time and have a few days off. Working on a weekly magazine means that you have to produce material week after week, 52 weeks a year and there is never a break, something I think few people appreciate, especially monthly magazine staff who often get a break by simply doing a double issue over Christmas and having a month off! 'If only,' I used to moan while I was editing weeklies. Now I am more than happy to churn out double the usual number of columns for a while, but it also means I need to get away for some peace and quiet — and that means the caravan.

Many women, including my mother, find it difficult to imagine a woman being alone in a caravan without worrying about intruders or being attacked. I think as a society we spend too much time indulging in fear rather than in reality. Yes, women are attacked but when you add it up the chances of that happening to any individual woman are very slim.

As the saying goes, 'There's more chance of being run over by a bus.' Statistics show that the leading killer of women in New Zealand is cancer, followed by heart disease, stroke, bronchitis and emphysema, diabetes, transport accidents, intentional self harm, pneumonia and influenza and hypertensive disease. Being murdered by a stranger while in a caravan (or anywhere else, for that matter) rates very low on that list.

If you led your life purely by what you read in the newspapers and watch on television you would never leave the house. That's because in most newsrooms around the country the maxim 'if it bleeds it leads' holds true, meaning that we have a plethora of stories every day that encourage us to hide in our houses and never leave. In the United States, the whole country seems to live on a daily diet of fear provided by their 24-hour television networks feeding them with near-miss terrorist attacks post-September 11. More people die every year as a result of the wars the United States military involves itself in, and many more people died in the Indian Ocean tsunami of 2004 than on September 11.

But the media still insist on running terror error reports, fanning the fear and incorrectly assuming that any event at an airport or train station is terrorist-led and linked to Osama Bin Laden.

Like my nana, I'm a big fan of getting a grip. But I'm also a defensive driver when it comes to steering my life, and I have taught my daughters to keep their wits about them and prevent nasty incidents before they happen. I think women should be able to feel safe because surely part of our fight for equality is the right to be able to spend time with ourselves without fear.

At our camp, the front gate is locked at night, so no one can drive in, but my dad did once comment rather ominously 'Yes, but you never know what might come up from the beach!' To this day I'm not sure if he meant alien sea creatures, James Bond, the SAS, the entire ANZAC Gallipoli forces or some guy looking to steal my kayak.

When I go to the caravan our big black huntaway/golden retriever cross, Shirl, comes too and she does a good impression of a guard dog if anyone she doesn't know pokes their head into the awning. I also lock the caravan up well, and I keep to myself rather than spending nights drinking with fellow campers I've just met. After all, I'm there for some silence, early nights and writing time. Even so, I occasionally lie awake, listening to the surf crash on the beach, cursing myself for reading a thriller before bed, or getting myself wound up about noises on the roof, that usually turn out to be possums.

One night Shirl and I were walking across a long stretch of grass to the ablution block when Shirl darted off into the bush. I assumed she had seen a rat or rabbit moving in there, but it turned out she was chasing something else. As I watched in the moonlight a large furry animal made its way across the grass in my direction with Shirl in hot pursuit.

It came straight at me and before I could say 'possum' it had climbed up my body and was sitting on my head. I didn't have time to wonder how hilarious a woman with a possum on her head must have looked. As the adrenalin kicked in, with one swift movement I grabbed the furry thing, which at the time seemed to be the size of a small dog, and hurled it onto the beach.

Shirl scrambled after it and returned about half an hour later with a big gash in her leg. I meanwhile stumbled off to the loo, had a nervous wee and then ran hell for leather back to the caravan and collapsed in a heap. Fortunately I had been wearing pyjamas so I didn't get any scratches from the possum's notoriously sharp claws. I rang Paul and blurted out the whole drama to him. He laughed his head off for a good five minutes.

The next morning, still in shock, I relayed the whole sorry tale during my regular Friday morning segment on Newstalk ZB. After Paul Holmes stopped laughing he said, 'It must have thought you were a big tree.'

'I may be tall,' I responded, 'but that's where the similarity with a tree ends.'

Then calls came flooding into the station from people saying that possums do indeed look for the tallest thing in sight when they are rushing from danger. I have since been known to crouch quite low on my way to the ablution block at night and I still have a little trouble sleeping if there's a possum on the roof.

For nights like those I turn to tart cherry syrup. My friend Kerre Woodham works on Newstalk ZB until midnight most nights and swears by the stuff. It calms you down and helps you sleep due to its high levels of melatonin. Our bodies produce melatonin naturally but stress and travel can reduce the amount we produce. The syrup also has antioxidants so I class it as a health food and it always helps me nod off. You can buy the syrup at health shops — just make sure you keep it in the fridge. About 30 ml of it diluted in water does the trick nicely for me.

Amidst the deadlines, the planting, the sheet whitening and the possums I almost forgot to worry about our time-wasting, non-laying hens. Then one morning I poked my head in the hen house and there it was. Our first egg. I let out a whoop of joy and cradled it in my hands immediately christening it 'Our First Egg'.

Paul came rushing out to the garden and we stood there gazing at it. A miracle to behold. When Pearl got home from school she picked it up gently, marvelling at its brown colour, its elliptical shape, its perfection.

'Who's going to eat it?' she asked.

'Oh you can,' I volunteered generously.

'No you have it,' she said.

'Paul, you have it,' I responded.

Having finally received our much-awaited first egg, it turned out we are all a bit squeamish about eating it. The delivery mechanism was just a little too close to home. Actually it was staring at us from just outside the kitchen door.

'It came out of her bum,' Pearl reminded us casting a wary look at Hillary in the backyard.

We were having our first lesson in the realities of self-sufficiency. Here were three people accustomed to buying their food hygienically packaged in sterile bags with pretty and informative labels. We put these packages in our car, drive them home and store them in our fridge. We have nothing to do with the slaughter of the animal which provided our steak, or the milking of the cow that provided the milk or the shelling of the oysters I have secretly stashed at the bottom of the trolley. Just the smells involved in all three of those processes would probably send this suburban family running for the hills and we're certainly not used to getting our food out of a bird's bum.

I could see that someone had to lead the way.

'Right I'll have it,' I said and charged out to the garden to gather the ingredients for what would become a frequent lunch dish from here on in, using a recipe I remember my dad cooking for me when I was a child. I sliced off a few leaves of silverbeet from the garden and brought them inside. I lightly steamed them while I poached the egg, which turned out to have a yolk the colour of saffron. I toasted some freshly-baked wholegrain bread, threw the drained spinach on the top and sat the lightly poached egg on top of that.

My husband and daughter watched eagerly as I broke into the yolk and let it run all over the silverbeet.

'Well?' they asked in unison as, with only a little rumble of nausea in my stomach, I raised a forkful to my mouth.

'I've never tasted anything so gorgeous in my life,' I grinned, yolky silverbeet poking out from behind my teeth.

I wasn't telling fibs. That egg – and all those that followed – consistently tasted better than any egg I have bought, even from a farmer's market. Each egg contains some of the purest protein you can find, a range of vitamins and important fatty acids, which contribute to the health of the brain and nervous system and help prevent heart disease. It is nature's perfect food. And we know exactly what went into ours, because it was us who fed our hens grains, lots of leftovers, alfalfa sprouts, slugs and bugs, weeds and their favourite green, silverbeet. They were created by hens that spend all day in the sunshine, scratching and digging, dust bathing, chasing each other and the cats, planning yet another escape mission and drinking clean fresh water. I regard them as our little powerhouses of clean, unadulterated nutrition and we eat every egg our chickens provide, which is usually three a day.

In months to come, however, there would be a week when I was unable to look at an egg. It was after a near-disastrous encounter with the thing that had put Pearl off trying Our First Egg: Hillary's bum.

Blueing Powder

Mix 3 cups of baking soda with half a teaspoon of Prussian Blue powder (you can get this pigment from art supply stores). Store in an airtight container.

For one set of sheets, add a teaspoon of the mixture to the final rinse of your wash, making sure the bowl is full first. If you're washing more than a set of sheets, increase the amount of blueing powder accordingly. If you hang your sheets out in direct sunlight, this will work even better. This is great for white shirts and underwear too.

Starch (for sheets, shirts and tablecloths)

Add the cooking water from pasta or potatoes into your final rinse to get sheets, shirts or tablecloths nice and crisp.

You can also mix 2 teaspoons of cornflour with a cup of water and put it in a spray bottle. Use this as a starch spray on your sheets while you are ironing them.

Lemon and Sunshine Stain Remover

For spot stain removal squeeze lemon juice onto the stain and then rub in some salt. Place the item on some grass in direct sunlight for as long as you can, then wash as normal. Your stain should have gone, if not repeat until it does.

Sesame-Lemon Dressing

This uses hardly any fat in return for a great flavour. Simply sprinkle half a teaspoon of sesame oil and the juice of a lemon over your salad. Flavour with some salt and pepper and toss. This also works really well on coleslaw – even the ones you buy prepared in plastic bags at the supermarket.

Body Oil

It is so easy to make a gorgeous body oil using your favourite essential oil. Find a carrier you like, such as almond, olive, wheatgerm, apricot kernel or jojoba oil. Mix 30 ml of this with 30 drops of your favourite essential oil. Lavender is great for relaxing after a night-time bath, ylang ylang is good if you have romance on your mind, or try rose geranium if you are a little pre-menstrual. Why not try mixing a few oils together to create your own signature scent?

Magic Night Cream

This takes a bit of getting used to because it's basically a salad dressing! But it does the job beautifully.

½ cup olive oil (extra virgin if you can afford it)

3 teaspoons apple cider vinegar (organic if you have it)

about 1 tablespoon water

3 drops lavender essential oil

Mix the olive oil and the cider vinegar. Add water slowly, mixing it until a smooth white/yellow cream forms. Add the lavender oil or any other essential oil you like the smell of to mask the salad dressing smell. You will need to give this a good shake before use every night as the mixture will settle. Store it in the fridge in a glass jar.

Balinese Jamu

4 tablespoons finely grated fresh turmeric (use a ginger grater)

1 tablespoon lime or lemon juice

2 teaspoons honey

Combine and drink every morning until you feel better.

DECEMBER

Iknow there are at least three ways to kill a chicken. I just wasn't sure which one I'd use when the time came – which could have been just a matter of days away.

Before Hillary, Yoko and Marigold arrived, I lived in a lovely old villa with lush, albeit a little overgrown and disordered, gardens front and back. Seemingly overnight my home felt like it had been transported to the most war torn and arid parts of Baghdad. Only the trees survived amidst the desert-like dust which now pervaded the garden. Three birds, each the size of a small bucket, were consuming 10 times their weight in plants and bugs a day.

I had become a prisoner in my own home, surrounded by green chicken wire and several make-shift gates, which involve hooking bits of wire around nails in a haphazard manner. Our outside living space was confined to a small deck and a veranda out the front. The rest had officially become chicken land. It gave me a new appreciation of just how the Palestinians feel.

When it comes to escaping, our hens are regular little Hogan's Heroes, compiling coded intelligence as they check out the perimeter of the fence for gaps while masquerading as chickens merely carrying on as chickens do. They've also trained the cats to squeeze under the fence thus creating a convenient chicken-sized gap, the location of which they record in their notebooks for later use.

'You wanted them to be free range,' my husband quite rightly argued as I wondered aloud how far you actually have to stretch the hen's neck before it would break.

'I had no idea of the sheer force of their destructive abilities and quite frankly I want my garden back.'

This would be the garden that now lives permanently under siege, protected only by some chicken wire and a series of mini-greenhouse tunnels. Tomato plants bravely produced fruit under fire, basil plants cautiously put out leaves, lettuces wilted gratefully in the heat of the tunnel. What used to be my lush garden now resembled a seed-trial laboratory.

'Wow, the flies are bad this year,' was a statement made by everyone lucky enough to get through the makeshift gate and out onto our deck.

'It's the chickens,' I would respond reaching for my home-made fly repellent and spraying it forcefully over their food, their drinks and their babies.

'Don't worry it's natural,' I assured them. 'Nothing but black tea and citronella.'

They would exchange looks that I now believe to mean 'they've totally lost the plot over those chickens' then politely leave clutching the fresh eggs that they really didn't want.

We would only have guests after dark, when flies hand over the job of terrorising humans to their good friends the mosquitoes and the hens are safely tucked up in their coop and I can pretend they don't exist.

My family, meanwhile, love the birds with a passion. Part of the chickens' invasion plan was to win over the people closest to me. They deliver three eggs a day in time for breakfast. Yoko even produces gigantic double yolkers, which delight Pearl every time. They come running and clucking, looking for all the world like loving pets, the minute they are called. Even the adult children, who are called in to mind them while we are at the caravan, confess to warm feelings of affection — and some of them don't even like eggs.

As I sulked and moaned and invented even more powerful natural fly sprays, the family called in a builder to get some proper fences and gates built 'so that it looks like we've always had hens and people don't have to tie bits of wire around nails anymore.'

Meanwhile, I was thinking a simple neck wringing after dark might be in order.

My December had not got off to a good start. But at least the hens, as much trouble as they are causing, were paying their way. I began to look sideways at the other animal members of our family and wonder out loud exactly what they contributed. In return for some grain and leftovers, the hens give us eggs. In return for some dog food and cat biscuits the dog and three cats give us . . . ?

'Why don't you just get it over with and write a children's story,' suggested Paul.

'About what?'

'About a horrible mother who kills all the pets in the home who don't contribute anything and then once they are dead realises that the home is over-run with rats and mice because there are no cats to kill them and the house gets burgled because the dog isn't there to protect it.'

'Finished?' I snapped before wandering off to submit a proposal to my publisher.

If I'm honest, Shirl is a great guard dog scaring couriers and good friends down the path and back into their cars on occasion. Like all old villas our house has a long hallway which leads to the front door and Shirl will hurl herself down that passage barking her head off at anything that appears at the entrance. In other respects she is very well trained to sit, lie down, come when called, and heel. She doesn't chase cats when we're walking and even stops at the side of the road and waits to be told if it is safe to cross. But it's very hard to train a dog out of doing what comes naturally, which is to protect its family. The best I have been able to do is train her to divert into our bedroom by the front door when she is in mid-hurl down the hallway. People still run away but it means that I can conveniently shut her in the bedroom before opening our front door.

As for the cats, only one catches rats and mice — the eldest, Kitty, who is a Grey Lynn native sired by a huge Persian grey and white tom who roamed the neighbourhood for years. She is extremely beautiful and knows it and, despite her large bulk, is surprisingly agile and fast when it comes to chasing down vermin. In November she rouses herself into nights of activity and neatly deposits baby rats and mice at the back door for us to find each morning. And then she takes the year off until the next November, preferring to curl up under the lime tree for the summer and by the fire for the winter.

Our other two cats, Lucy and Sassy, who we adopted after they were abandoned at the side of the road, rarely leave the property. Lucy is not right in the head and never has been, which is understandable because when she was found someone had attempted to slit her throat. The vet fixed her up but she wouldn't go near men for years and is still prone to major fits of anxiety, usually brought on by Kitty, who loves nothing better than to corner her and give her a good beating. Sassy is just a bit lazy. She likes to sit on the fence with both hind legs hanging down the sides like you see lions do in the jungle.

Thanks to the hens, our place soon became home to a colony of rats, who by all accounts were having a grand old time at Chez Wendyl, situated just a stone's throw from regular food scraps and hen pellet detritus. They took up residence underneath our lounge floor and made so much noise that we had to turn up the TV during *Coronation Street*, even when Gail and Eileen were in full fish-wife mode, screeching at each other across the cobblestones.

The rats seemed to spend most of their time tickling each other. At least that's what I discovered after researching the reason they screech so much. Apparently rats mostly communicate like dolphins, using ultrasonic communications not audible to the human ear. But they screech, presumably for our benefit, when they are involved in massive tickling sessions and a bit of sex.

'Where did you read that? Believeanything.com?' Paul scoffed.

'I think it's rather sweet,' I responded insisting on humanising the pests, as I do the pets.

I didn't think it was so sweet, however, when I looked out the window one afternoon and saw a rat the size of a cat casually wandering around my back deck.

The next day I went out and got rat poison from my local Mitre 10, where my usual sales assistant hooted out loud at the first product I intended to buy. It had the words 'eco' and 'natural' on it.

'What do you think is natural about killing a rat?' she asked me.

'I don't know, it just makes me feel better.'

She rolled her eyes, as once again, the eco marketing had lulled me into believing I was not really killing rats at all, just sort of.

We worked out that there was little difference between my eco brand and the real deal and after much discussion I left with some severe looking rat poison much against my green, environmentally-friendly principals. She also sold me a rat trap which you set with peanut butter ('just in case you really want to live like your nana'). I didn't hold out much hope, as I had already bought a rat trap which was supposed to zap them with an electrical current, killing them humanely and instantly. To date, neither trap has caught a rat but the poison worked fairly swiftly. We had sick, dying rats staggering all over the property for days afterwards and Paul had to be summoned with the spade to end their misery. Judging by the smell that fogged into our lounge after the rats climbed back into their nest to die, and decompose, we got them all.

The smell was so bad we couldn't watch *Coro St* for two weeks. No one was willing to go and have a look for the nest so we just cordoned off the lounge, like they do a crime scene. It certainly smelled like a crime scene.

At least the garden looked magnificent by December. The combination of warmer weather, plenty of spring rain and longer days had meant the plants were all thriving and giving the back of my house a very productive feel.

Unfortunately these conditions also help bugs and fungus to thrive. I am always on the alert for early blight on my tomatoes and work hard to keep lower growth trimmed to allow plenty of air circulating around the plants. It is too early for the green shield bug which will make itself felt in vast numbers later in the summer but I can already see their young, the little black bugs with spots on their backs.

When it comes to pest control I have a very relaxed attitude. I try to garden organically but what really is organic? To be an organic purist I would have to change all my soil, which has been fertilised with non-organic blood and bone on occasion. I would also have to make all my seed organic before I raised it, which means I would have to ditch all the seed I have lovingly collected over the years. I probably shouldn't throw on horse dung, which I collect from the roadside in Matamata, because I can't be sure that the horses were fed only organic feed.

You can see how it starts to get complicated and I wonder what the advantages are to being strictly organic if it means I have to pay good money and work hard to find organic compounds, when I know that the produce I am growing is not only economical but good for me and chemical free. I'm more interested in words like 'sustainable,' 'nutritious' and 'accessible' than 'organic'.

Instead I prefer to stick to a few basic rules. I don't use chemical pesticides or insecticides on my plants and I fertilise with organic liquid seaweed fertiliser and blood and bone. This means that by the time we eat our garden produce I can be sure that, for the most part, no chemicals have been added to it or used to kill off beneficial insects like bees, ladybirds and praying mantises.

But when my lemon tree was attacked by lemon-tree borer I went out and bought a can full of poison and injected it into the tree. I had tried natural methods like poking the holes the borer had formed in the trunk with a bit of wire and pouring some turps down it, but they returned. I love my Yen Ben lemon tree which I planted three years ago and I'm sorry but I'm not letting some borer kill it. From now on I guess my lemons will not be organic, but at least they will still be there.

Keeping bugs and disease away is tough without chemicals but there are some really basic things you can do which simply require a little bit of effort on your part. Early detection is important so inspect plants daily. Many bugs can be picked off by hand, or in the case of aphids brushed off with a toothbrush. You can also give a tomato plant a good shake to dislodge bugs – and in my case the hens run around underneath and gobble them all up. You can also encourage good insects, such as ladybirds and praying mantises, by not using anything in the garden that might kill them as well as your intended victim. Most commercially bought insecticides will kill all the insects on your plants including the beneficial ones.

I also work hard to encourage birds into my garden by putting food out on feeders and providing large trees at the front of my house for them to nest in. At last count we have a pair of blackbirds who nest every year in the tree around the side of the house, and a pair of wax-eyes who produce a loud bunch of chicks right outside my bedroom window where I can check on them every morning in the spring and watch their babies. There's also another pair of wax-eyes in the puriri tree. In the evenings they make a circuit of my property and pick insects off my vege patch as part of their nightly routine.

Crop rotation is also important as a way to eliminate disease and insects because during the cold months fungal spores and insect larvae overwinter in the soil and plant litter, ready to emerge and attack the same plant in the spring. But if the same plant isn't there because you've planted corn instead of cabbage they will not thrive.

At the first sign of blight on my tomatoes I whip out the copper oxychloride and spray them every few weeks – some organic growers frown on using this. As a guide for spraying plants, if the container you're holding has a label that advises a withholding period before harvesting, don't use it. There are chemicals in it that can be harmful, which is why they don't want you to eat the vegetable until the chemicals have dispersed.

I have many recipes for various sprays, some of which you will find at the end of the chapter but my favourite find is neem oil. It is used in India in soaps, toothpaste and cosmetics, is non toxic to mammals and beneficial insects, and is also biodegradable. You can buy neem oil at some garden centres and it is fantastic in the garden because it has so many uses. It makes plants unpalatable to insects, but if they still attack it has a growth regulator, which inhibits their ability to molt and lay eggs. It is great on your roses for aphids and elsewhere in the garden for leafminers, mealy bugs, thrips and whitefly. You do need to apply quite a lot of it, though. I recommend spraying with it in the morning and the evening every few weeks.

Diatomaceous earth works well as a dust to control crawling pests like slugs and snails and on plants it will kill aphids and caterpillars. It is a naturally occurring silicon powder that you can apply around the base of seedlings and lightly dust foliage. Do avoid inhaling the particles as the silica can aggravate lungs, so wear a dust mask. It can also be used to control mites and fleas on our animals.

And for slugs and snails, no natural garden is complete without a slug trap. You can buy these at garden centres, or you can simply use a saucer submerged in the soil. I fill the trap with stale beer and am rewarded with dead, previously drunk, snails and slugs, which I then feed to my appreciative hens.

Another way to keep your garden healthy is to view it as

a living breathing community. If one of my plants just isn't keeping up or is obviously in poor health I dig it up and burn it. It may sound harsh but spending money on fertilisers and sprays probably isn't going to help. By eliminating weak plants and their weak genes from my garden I am encouraging a stronger strain of plants.

As Christmas Day approaches in my house there are three things that need attending to. First is Christmas spirit. When it comes to Christmas spirit I need to have a long, hard think about my attitude, according to Pearl.

My disinclination to 'dress' the house for the Christmas season with tinsel, fairy lights and a neon Santa complete with reindeer on the roof causes problems most years. This year my insistence that we reject the tradition of killing a pine tree so that we can watch it slowly die in the living room in favour of one I have had growing in a pot in the front garden all year was seen as nothing short of heresy.

'She's doing it again,' I overheard Pearl say to Paul.

'Don't worry, I'll sort it,' he replied shortly before he did something with his hands which I can only assume is some sort of Homie G street sign for 'be cool'. Or in his case, 'be cool even if I'm too old to do street signs with my gnarly old hands'.

This is not new territory for Paul as he has spent the past 15 years attempting to instil in me some sort of celebratory spirit around the Christmas season. Every year enormous trees are sacrificed and whole days are set aside for decorating it with heirloom decorations. Heirloom decorations? Who makes heirlooms out of baubles, stars and tinsel? I just don't get it.

Tables begin groaning with Christmas delicacies weeks before the actual day and children are whipped up into an anticipatory fever.

When we had Pearl I accused Paul of child abuse when, year after year, he dragged the poor poppet to the mall to get the 'traditional family picture with Santa.' He would return with a petrified child and a picture of her crying her eyes out in terror on the lap of some sweaty guy in a Santa suit.

Her first Christmas was such a production — with her four older siblings in starring roles — that halfway through opening her presents she cried weakly, 'No more Santa!'

'Hilarious!' he said.

Finally, Pearl succumbed and became Daddy's little Christmas fairy who sees it as her mission from that first taste of cheap chocolate gleaned from her advent calendar on 1 December to 'create a magical Christmas'.

And a living tree in a pot does not a magical Christmas make.

'Why don't you like Christmas?' Pearl asked. 'Everyone likes Christmas.'

'It's not that I don't like it,' I replied. 'I just can't be bothered with all the fuss and the materialism. And I think you'll find that the real meaning of Christmas is about being with family, not how much tinsel you can cram into one house.'

Then we went outside to look at the tree in the pot I had been growing all year. It had let me down badly and stood barely half a metre tall.

She gave me a look I recognised with horror as the clever one I use to express the sentiment of 'Oh come on, get a grip.'

And so a two-metre Christmas tree was fetched and carried and erected.

Now we just needed to make the hampers. Over the years we have turned away from buying all our relatives ridiculous presents they do not want or use. This year we decided to start the tradition of making hampers. I used to think making gifts for people was a bit corny. This probably came from my childhood in the '60s and '70s when my parents were in the grip of new consumerism leaving behind their own childhoods when times had been tough, food scarce and, by necessity, gifts were handmade. My grandfather used to send us birthday and Christmas cards which were recycled. He would cut the picture off the front of an old card and glue it to some new card. I remember thinking how extraordinarily uncool this was as a child, but now it seems to be a sensible and thoughtful thing to do.

I think people have grown tired of quick-fix presents bought in a hurry from a shopping mall. Instead something that tastes good, made by someone they love strikes a special chord on Christmas Day. The real secret is making it taste good. If you can't cook then don't try making preserves, perhaps turn your hand to something along the lines of handcrafts or potted plants.

This Christmas we simply assembled our favourite recipes from the past year and spent our free time in the kitchen cooking with a few glasses of wine and lots of music blaring. I made green peppercorn mustard, chilli jam, Worcestershire sauce, pumpernickel bread and Paul made his famous herbed salt.

I disappeared into our store room, which used to be a bedroom, and unearthed jars I had collected from op shops throughout the year. I gave them a good clean and sterilise before filling them with my freshly made recipes. Before long our kitchen table heaved with jars and jars of our favourite kitchen staples that were then packaged up with eggs from the hens and some chocolates (not homemade).

'They look really good,' said Pearl, who had helped me arrange everything on platters I found on a quick raid of an op shop. The platters were then covered with straw.

'They do don't they?' I said, standing back with my hands on my hips, regretting having the thought —while I was stirring yet another batch of chilli jam — that it would have been a lot easier, and probably cheaper, to go to Kmart and buy 12 boxes of assorted biscuits.

'Time well spent,' said Paul, reading my mind. 'And a gift which says so much more than a box of biscuits,' he grinned.

Later we celebrated the end of our hamper making with a glass of wine at the kitchen table, as we do most nights while one of us cooks and the other chats. Paul pointed out that the hamper exercise had been great for Pearl to realise that Christmas isn't just about offloading hundreds of dollars at a shopping mall. One of the many lessons Pearl has had from us that her older four siblings never got because we were both rushing around editing magazines and falling into bed exhausted having arrived home at 6 pm, fed four children, supervised homework, and put three loads of washing on.

In return we have a child who appreciates good food with a distinct Italian flair. We reason that this came from a trip to Europe we made in December a few years ago with all five children. It was nearly Paul's fiftieth birthday and all he wanted to do was give our kids the gift of travel. He also wanted them to realise early in life that there was a whole other world out there. A world that is completely different and culturally ancient compared to New Zealand. So we took them all to Paris for Christmas.

We rented out three tiny apartments and spent a mad week together taking in art, gorgeous food and wandering around Versailles on a freezing cold winter's day. Daniel and Hannah carried on to Barcelona where they stayed with their aunty, and Joel and Alex flew home. Paul and I carried on to Italy with Pearl, who was eight at the time.

When we arrived in Sicily we were a little frazzled. We had caught the wrong train and ended up miles away from Syracuse where we were supposed to be. The Italian train system is fantastic but getting any sense out of conductors and ticket offices can be quite difficult if you don't speak Italian. When we finally found our apartment it was in a very old, run-down building by the water. The streets around the apartment were awash with a sea of old vegetables and ice that were being cleaned up by noisy men with brooms in overalls and gumboots.

'Surely this isn't the place?' I mumbled as we rang a bell and peered through the broken glass.

Almost immediately, a vibrant red-head called Ida took us up in the cranky old lift to her wonderful apartment where she fed us and helped us plan our stay. The apartment we rented from Ida had the most beautiful views out over the water, but most importantly we looked straight down on the daily food market, which snaked around our building. Pearl and I visited every day marvelling at the different kinds of fish and the incredible variety of fresh vegetables and fruits. Purple and green broccoli, white and yellow cauliflower, celeriac, bunches of fresh new carrots and radishes, courgettes, peppers, tomatoes and of course Sicilian oranges. I wished we were staying somewhere with a kitchen so that I could join the many Italians who arrived with their shopping trundlers and bought their food daily. Throughout our stay in Sicily we couldn't help noticing how keen the Sicilians were to introduce Pearl to new foods. She was always being offered tastes of this and that in restaurants and on our last morning our landlady had baked a cake especially for Pearl to take on our long bus-trip to Palermo.

We had to wait a few hours for the bus to turn up – we had been given the wrong time – and as we huddled in the cold on the corner an old man walked past and commented on Pearl's white blonde hair. At least I think that's what he said as I heard the word 'bellissimo' in there somewhere.

Moments later he returned with a gift for her. He placed in her hands a brown paper bundle which contained a freshly baked ciabatta roll filled with prosciutto and cheese. It smelled gorgeous and Pearl devoured the whole thing on the spot. We thanked the man profusely and left Sicily with a lasting impression of old-world people who eat fresh food every day and regard it as something to be treasured.

Since that day Pearl has developed a distinctly Italian passion for food and will beg us to buy her prosciutto, goat's feta and pesto whenever we are in a food store that stocks them. She will also try any new food, open to finding a new discovery. Her most recent find was green olives from, you guessed it, Sicily. We're happy to pay the price for them reasoning that they are better for her than the junk others her age – and her four siblings used to – consume. And thanks to Sicily we have a child who can taste and appreciate the best food has to offer.

There was only one more thing I had to do before Christmas and that was head down to the caravan to set it up for the family. Every year we go down there to avoid those mad few days before Christmas when Auckland turns into a heaving mass of traffic with frustrated, overtired people trying to finish work and get their Christmas shopping done. We set up our awning, give the caravan a good scrub, put the tent up for extra guests and head home on Christmas Eve. Paul and I won't be at the caravan over the holidays. It's far too busy for us. Christmas and New Year belongs to our kids and their many friends who converge on the camp and fill our normally quiet old caravan with one big party.

This year, we spent Christmas Eve back in town, as

always, with the kids, drinks, homemade pizza and *The Last Waltz*. Paul's kids, Alex and Joel, gave him the DVD years ago. We all fell in love with the Martin Scorsese documentary of The Band's last concert featuring astonishing performances by Joni Mitchell, Van Morrison, Neil Young, Dr John, Eric Clapton, Emmylou Harris, Muddy Waters, Bob Dylan and The Staple Singers.

Kids, nieces and any of their friends who are at a loose end have dinner with us and then we all settle down in the lounge to watch *The Last Waltz*. After the first run through the trouble starts.

'Play Van again!' someone shouts.

'No, Joni!'

'No, Neil!'

And it goes on all night as we wrestle the remote off each other and someone (usually Hannah) is forced to step in as adjudicator to make sure all requests are treated fairly and equally.

At some point, Pearl slopes off to bed, resigned to the fact that her entire family are a little worse for wear and knowing it's best she saves her energy for the morning's present unwrapping.

By midnight we are still replaying, singing along, a little tiddly and a little loud. It is possibly the one night of the year when my neighbours could legitimately call noise control.

Finally, we all stumble off to bed, humming to ourselves and ready to wake early for Christmas Day and the arrival of Lila and her parents bright and early.

This year my son Daniel didn't come on Christmas Eve.

'I want to start Christmas Day without a hangover,' he said.

'Good idea,' I responded and helped myself to another glass of bubbles.

The next day I wished I had followed his lead as I woke early to get the Christmas bread roll dough out of the fridge where it had been sitting all night, waiting to be kneaded and baked into warm, sweet, doughy parcels. Paul sliced the ham he had glazed the day before with orange, mustard and clove and we fried up our hens' eggs with sausages, tomatoes and mushrooms.

'Breakfast!' we announced to Daniel, Holly, Hannah, Alex, Joel, Gemma, Mariko, Adam, Pearl and Lila – our family, partners and their children.

'Perfect,' said Paul mumbling through a mouth of ham and eggs.

'Lovely,' I answered, bouncing Lila on my knee and handing her another piece of Christmas roll.

Herbed Salt

4 heaped tablespoons fresh rosemary

4 heaped tablespoons fresh thyme

2 heaped tablespoons fresh oregano or marjoram

12 peeled garlic cloves

500 grams sea salt

Finely chop the herbs and garlic. Mix with salt in a large
bowl and let stand for 24 hours at room temperature to
dry out. (the smell in your kitchen is amazing!) Place
in an airtight container. This salt is best sprinkled
on steak before cooking and patted all over a chicken
before roasting with a bit sprinkled inside. You can also
use it to season pasta sauces and it's delicious sprinkled
on tomatoes on toast.

Chilli Jam

4 cloves garlic, peeled and chopped

1 tablespoon ginger, peeled and chopped

3 fresh chillies, chopped

1 teaspoon cumin seeds

1 teaspoon brown mustard seeds

50 ml red wine vinegar

500g tomatoes, chopped (preferably fresh but tinned will do)

1 tablespoon fish sauce

75g brown sugar or palm sugar

½ tablespoon turmeric powder

handful of coriander, chopped

In a food processor or mortar and pestle, grind the garlic, ginger, chillies, cumin, mustard seeds and red wine vinegar to a paste. Transfer to a heavy bottomed saucepan, then add the tomatoes, fish sauce, sugar and turmeric.

Simmer over a low heat for 40 minutes until it resembles a sauce. Fold through the coriander at the last minute and put into jars while hot.

Worcestershire Sauce

2.5 cups malt vinegar

500 grams treacle

1 teaspoon salt

1.5 cm piece green ginger, finely chopped

2 cloves garlic, finely chopped

1 tablespoons ground cloves

½ teaspoon cayenne pepper

½ teaspoon ground cardamom (optional)

½ teaspoon ground black pepper

Combine all the ingredients in a saucepan. Bring to the boil and cook gently uncovered for 20 minutes. Cover and let stand overnight. Next day, strain and bottle.

Green Peppercorn Mustard

1 cup yellow mustard seeds

4 tablespoons green peppercorns, rinsed (you can buy big jars of these at
   Asian supermarkets, bulk bin stores and Indian grocers)

4 cloves garlic, crushed

1 cup oil

2 cups white wine vinegar (tarragon or rosemary are good too)

2 teaspoons salt

Combine all the ingredients in a bowl and leave to
stand in a cool place for two days. Don't leave it any
longer, as I once did, or it goes off and tastes dreadful!
In a blender mix the mustard until you have a coarse
paste. You may need to do this in batches. Mix the
blended mustard well and spoon into small, clean jars.
Melt over some sealing wax, filling right to the top of
the jar.

Ham Glaze

juice of 1 orange

1 cup liquid honey

2 tablespoons wholegrain mustard

cloves

Blend process or hand-whisk juice of one orange plus a cup of honey and a couple of tablespoons of wholegrain mustard. Carefully trim the skin off the ham, leaving as much thick fat as possible. Use a sharp knife to make a criss-cross pattern in the fat, being careful not to cut right through to the meat. Where the lines cross stud with whole cloves. Put ham in a large baking dish then pour over the orange juice mixture. Put in a cool oven, around 120C° and baste again every 10 minutes until the ham is a bright golden brown, which should be in about an hour.

Wendyl's Safe Fly Spray

8 ml citronella oil

2 teaspoons washing-up liquid

1 tablespoon methylated spirits

2 tablespoons white vinegar

150 ml strong tea

850 ml water

Mix together and add water. Pour into a spray bottle and set it on a reasonably concentrated spray. You can also spray this on your skin as an insect repellent.

Aphid Spray

Dissolve one tablespoon of baking soda in hot water and then add one tablespoon each of dishwashing liquid, vegetable oil and liquid plant food. Add this mixture to 5 litres of water and spray every two days for a week and then every two weeks as a maintenance dose.

Oxalis Weed Killer

Fill a 1 litre spray bottle with white vinegar to which you add a teaspoon of baking soda and a teaspoon of dishwashing detergent. Spray on the weed and let dry. Repeat if necessary.

Natural Bug Spray

3–4 whole chilli peppers

3–4 cloves of garlic

½ cup water

¼ cup liquid detergent (I use Dr Bronner's castile soap)

enough water to fill remainder of spray bottle

Steep the chilli and garlic in the water over a low heat for 15 minutes. Cool and then pour into a spray bottle with liquid detergent. Fill the rest of the bottle with water. Spray on plants every two days for a week and then every two weeks as a maintenance dose.

Bug Spray

Collect a good handful of the insect pests that are causing damage — I use an old Agee jar with a piece of paper spread over the top, with a hole just big enough to pop the bugs through. Put the live or dead bugs in a kitchen blender with about two cups of water and blend at high speed until the insects are reduced to a pulp. Strain through a piece of cloth, and then dilute 1:4 with water. Spray on the foliage. The smell deters the insects. You may need to spray a few times before you get rid of them.

Or you can simply crush a few to death and leave them lying around as a deterrent.

Baking Soda Fungus Spray

Dissolve a teaspoon of baking soda in 1 litre of warm water. Add a teaspoon of liquid dishwashing soap and spray infected plants thoroughly making sure you cover the underside of the leaves.

JANUARY

I can't remember the last time I stayed up until midnight on New Year's Eve. It's dreadfully Nana of me but Paul and I tend to have a quiet night where we cook something lovely for dinner and then head off to bed. We like to try out a new recipe we've found in a Nigel Slater or Peter Gordon recipe book or clipped from a magazine – something involving duck or crab, a bit exotic and time consuming that we will have fun trying to cook and then devour later with a good bottle of chilled champagne. One year I decided to make mozzarella cheese for some reason and spent the whole day searching supermarkets for rennet. I ended up with something resembling cottage cheese and have never tried to make it again. However, I have since mastered two great recipes for cottage cheese and ricotta, which I don't make on New Year's

Eve! Once you have tried them, you'll never go back to that watery stuff they sell in the supermarkets.

I have to be at the Newstalk ZB studios for work on New Year's Day by 8 am for my nine-to-noon show and I prefer to do that with a clear head. This year we were babysitting Lila so we popped around to our friends Sido and Conrad for a quick New Year's Eve drink while Lila attempted to eat the entire contents of a bowl of dip before we headed back home for dinner.

Down at the caravan it is a different story. The camp will be chockablock, the parties will have started early and there will be a night of revelry unlike any other. Most of our children are down there with their friends and this year we will not make the mistake of turning up on New Year's Day to stay. One year we arrived down to about 20 hung-over young adults and set about feeding them, as you do. I made pizza bread, which is always a favourite with the kids, Paul got a barbecue going and Hannah, Daniel, Alex and Holly helped make a huge salad, gathering together bits and pieces provided by all the kids.

We had just laid a veritable feast out in the awning and everyone had managed to squeeze into a place to start eating when a girl I didn't know piped up:

'Do you have anything gluten free? I'm intolerant,' she said full of importance.

I sipped my wine and caught a look of despair from Hannah.

'Well darling,' I said in my nicest voice. 'There's some rice in the cupboard, you are most welcome to boil some up.'

She didn't. Perhaps she was cooking intolerant too.

We now delay our arrival at the camp until well after New Year's Day by which time the needy, gluten-free types have returned to the safety of their loving parents and the numbers have dwindled substantially.

If I'm honest, I don't enjoy the camp when it is busy. I'm lucky that I get to use it during the week throughout the year and not just at traditional holiday times. I find that after my year of living quietly, being crammed in with people and cars all around is quite claustrophobic. I am used to being at the camp during the week with the lovely retired couples occupying themselves with fishing, reading, sleeping and walks. I even liked the one old couple who used to run up and down the beach putting on a remarkable show of strength. I have even seen some having cuddles and tickling each other, which gives me hope for my retirement plans. My parents are typical of these old couples, happy to potter around the caravan, dozing off over a book and setting out on occasional shopping trips to town.

Old couples make great neighbours when I am working and want some time on my own. They are from the generation that respects your privacy and wouldn't dare intrude unless invited.

I wish all campers were like that. My bond with my caravan was nearly severed one year when I was mobbed by nosy parkers. It seemed not an hour would pass when someone didn't poke their nose around the awning and say 'You're Wendyl aren't you? I've heard you on the radio.' They would then quiz me on the private lives of popular broadcasters.

They weren't at all interested in me, thank goodness, but because I worked with people like Mike Hosking, Paul Holmes and Kerre Woodham, I seemed to be fair game for giving them a dose of star power.

'It's as if they think I live in Auckland in a house like *Big Brother* with Mike, Paul and Kerre and they all sit around sharing their innermost secrets with me and then I come down to the camp specifically to share those with anyone who cares to ask,' I groaned to my family.

Instead I would stand there awkwardly in my caravan doing my best to deflect the intruders with statements such as 'I wouldn't know, I really don't know him that well,' and 'Oh I haven't heard that at all,' and 'I'm sorry to disappoint you, I just work with them.'

Finally, after a particularly harrowing week of it, I was packing up to go home when someone decided that standing in my awning wasn't enough of a personal space invasion. They stood in the doorway and wouldn't shut up. I was a prisoner in my own caravan on the receiving end of 20 questions about Mike Hosking. Paul was outside packing the car so he rang me on my cell phone to give me a reason to get away from the conversation politely. I think he may have sensed that I was about to slam the door in the intruder's face, which was true.

I was so upset that my haven, my place of peace had suddenly become a free for all for anyone who wished to rock up and ask me about things that were none of their business — or mine, for that matter.

'That's it, I'm not coming back,' I said rather petulantly to my father.

'You can't blame them,' he said reasonably. 'You're a name they know on the radio. They think that you are that friendly, likeable, chatty person all the time,' he sniggered.

'Dad, it's not me they want to talk to. It's the people I know and quite frankly that is offensive.'

'I think you need to take a deep breath and take these people for who they are. Nice, country people who like a chat. We're Aucklanders, we don't often understand that it is different down here. Conversation is an art and art takes time.'

I knew about Aucklanders versus the rest of New Zealand. We had been very lucky to be accepted in our campground and we rarely see other big city dwellers there, which makes it a very pleasant place to be. Occasionally, though, we do find it difficult to blend in, especially when we are trying to master the forces of nature.

Paul once bought a pair of swimming shorts which I'm sure he thought were just lovely when he paid $1.50 for them at an op shop, but the bright red and yellow colours made him look like a surf lifesaver. The first time he wore them I told him that the surf lifesavers had rung and said they wanted their pants back.

'Funny you should say that,' he replied not skipping a beat. 'Someone just asked me if I was a lifesaver while I was out on the kayak.'

That'll be the yellow and red kayak, which matches his yellow and red shorts.

'Looking forward to your first rescue,' I muttered as I stalked off to go fishing.

Little did I know how soon that rescue would be.

I had spent a harrowing few hours attempting to cast a line off the beach using my new left-handed reel and rod. I hadn't realised it was left-handed until I did my first right-handed cast, so I simply told myself that for the purposes of fishing I would now become ambidextrous.

There I was casting my line in an odd right-handed/left-handed fashion when I was joined by the locals. When it comes to fishing, the locals are generally patient and understanding of the disability of being an Aucklander. According to them, we are hopeless at everything from erecting tents to lighting barbecues and we apparently even swim funny. The locals are good looking men. Big and muscle bound, fans of the black singlet, friendly enough, even if it is just to ascertain that once again I was using the wrong bait, fishing at the wrong end of the tide and casting into the wrong part of the water.

'But don't worry,' said the shorter one. 'We're here now, the fish will come soon.'

'Thanks,' I said, noting the glint of sarcasm in his eyes.

They then set about fishing with such expertise and grace that I was immediately intimidated and began hitting myself in the head with my sinker, tripping over my line and piercing myself with my own fish hooks.

The locals exchanged a look. As it wafted past I sniffed its meaning. 'Another bloody Aucklander.'

Which is when my surf lifesaver decided to paddle over on his kayak for a visit.

'God,' I said under my breath as I saw him jauntily heading in my direction paddling in his enthusiastic style which involves the boat zigzagging its way forward rather than choosing a more direct route. 'Please no.'

God was obviously busy elsewhere because in a jiffy there he was right in front of us, a huge smile on his face shouting: 'A drink for my darling fisherwoman! Corona or Crown Lager my sweet?'

The shame of it all. I thought I saw a local snigger shortly before his mate began to laugh out loud.

I encouraged Paul to pull the boat in away from our eager audience and we sat and drank our beers on the sand, which is when I decided it would be nice to float back across the estuary to the caravan while he towed me in the kayak.

As we plunged headlong into the outgoing current my husband paddled and paddled and we didn't move an inch. In fact we began to move backwards, swept out to sea by a current which went right past the locals and into huge surf.

'Ah . . . the current darling,' I shouted to Paul who

85

was still paddling fervently, oblivious to the fact that his wife was doing a good impression of a sea anchor. Then in an attempt to sound like our fast exit into the surf was entirely for the locals' benefit, I shouted. 'What a great ride!' as I faced certain death.

We were goners. I cursed myself. I knew this current and I should have known better.

Which is when I had the foresight to stand up — in what revealed itself to be water so deep and turbulent that it came all the way up to my knees.

The locals looked at me. I looked at them. We all had a laugh.

The Great Siege of the Mike Hosking Fan occurred shortly afterwards, providing a double whammy of reasons not to love the caravan.

I went away and sulked. I avoided the caravan for a few months as I tried to figure out how to deal with the problem. On the one hand I could just be rude and say something like: 'Look, I talk for a living, I'm here to relax and get some peace and quiet so if you wouldn't mind . . . ' but I didn't want to reinforce their prejudices. I come from a city where people are not known for their warmth and personality. We are seen as busy individuals who spend all day in traffic jams abusing each other. And when we're not doing that we're sitting in cafes drinking chardonnay and gossiping about our materialistic lives. None of which is too far from the truth.

Finally I worked out what to do. Much to Pearl and Paul's amusement I cast a spell. It's something I learned to do when I was training to be a celebrant. During the course, one of the more spiritual members of the course gave a spell-making demonstration.

I wandered around the perimeter of my caravan and sprinkled salt saying over and over in my head: 'Please respect my privacy and let me be.'

'Mum, I think you're supposed to sprinkle salt not grind it out of the salt grinder,' interrupted Pearl.

'I don't have any, this will have to do.' I snapped.

Then I sprinkled cleansing lavender oil. Then I lit candles.

The only problem was that we then bundled ourselves back into the car and drove home to Auckland – leaving the candles alight on dry grass on a hot January afternoon.

Fortunately my long-suffering father was there to douse them.

'I really think you're over-reacting,' he said quite reasonably.

I then decided that from now on I would simply be firm, but not rude. I remembered Paul Holmes once telling me in an interview years ago that while he loved talking to his fans who came up to him on the street, if you stopped, you were stuck and it was hard to get away. So when people came up to talk to him he just kept walking. The idea is to be pleasant but never stop, or you'll be there forever.

There I was, years later, using a device to avoid talking about Paul Holmes, told to me by Paul Holmes, who uses it to avoid talking about himself.

And it worked, even if it meant that I was always just off to the loo, or the kitchen, or the moon. Only once did I find myself crouching down inside the caravan while Paul dealt with a stranger who had wandered up and announced himself with the words: 'So this is where Wendyl is. I've heard her on the radio with that Mike Hosking, what a pillock.. . . is she about?' Paul told him I was in the loo and said he'd pass on his regards. Pearl spent the whole two minutes giggling like a loon.

I work most of January at Newstalk ZB doing the holiday shows where people ring up and ask advice from our experts who sit with me in the studio. I've been doing the shows for nearly 10 years now and I find them extremely enjoyable. I always come back from a show armed with new knowledge from one of my guests or a caller. It can be on anything from getting rid of lemon tree borer to how to make your jam set.

This year my boss, Bill Francis, asked me to do a few sessions on my own answering calls about my Green Goddess tips. The first show I did, I was delighted to see the board light up with callers even before I'd gone to air and the hour rocked along at a great pace, which was a blessing. There is nothing worse than sitting in a studio and having no one to talk to on a talkback station. It is great for me to work out what demand there is out there for my cleaning recipes and also to get some tips from some of the older listeners.

After one of my Green Goddess shows I came home and invented a cleaning paste for bathroom and kitchen sinks. I used to just sprinkle baking soda and mix it with a bit of water but a woman who called up said she liked to have a paste already made, like Jif. It got me thinking and I mixed cream of tartar, baking soda, some liquid castile soap and peppermint oil to make my own cleaning paste. It smells amazing and works well.

I also decided to take to my books to try to find an alternative laundry detergent. My lavender laundry liquid is being made by lots of people all over New Zealand, I know because they email me to say how much they love it. You can make it with castile soap, which is the green option, or it works really well with good old Sunlight soap. The problem is that Sunlight has beef tallow and ethylenediaminetetraaceticacid (EDTA) which is a known pollutant. That said, I was relieved to find out from the company that makes the soap that their palm oil is derived from a sustainable source. The recipe (see page 274) calls for half a bar of Sunlight soap and makes about eight litres, which is enough for 128 machine loads. This level of dilution means that the amount of nasties the recipe uses is a lot less than used in commercial products.

Despite the popularity of my lavender laundry liquid, I was still keen to make a laundry powder. I sourced some liquid castile soap and fiddled around for a day or two with my old favourites baking soda, washing soda and lavender oil. The result was a laundry clay. It looks just like white clay, so that is what I've called it. My first test washes with it astounded me. Paul's dirty jeans came out as clean as a whistle. It has continued to impress me as it passed the 'no white powder marks on black clothes' test and the 'no foaming, so it can be used in front loaders' test.

'They really like this Nana stuff,' I said to Paul when I got home after my last show for the season.

'You're the new Aunty Daisy,' he joked.

'Well, not quite. I'm a bit more modern than that.'

'No, you're not. You're using everything she did and you are getting the same sort of listeners,' he said.

To a certain extent he is right. Through my columns in the *New Zealand Woman's Weekly* and the shows on Newstalk ZB, I have sensed a real need and desire by women to return to the old ways, to make do, to reject modern convenience and get back to the heart of the family.

I picked up one of my old Aunt Daisy books and opened it at the foreword and read how Daisy Basham welcomed her listeners on 1ZB with the words 'Good *morning* everybody!' at 9 am every day. She never wrote a script but instead would just chat with her listeners passing on hints and recipes shared by the radio community she created from 1936 until her last broadcast in June 1963. Hers was an astonishing career during which time she wrote many books, one of which has recently been re-released.

One thing I never see mentioned in the old books like Aunt Daisy's is sunscreen. Obviously the link between sunlight and skin cancer had not been made but at the same time the idea of sitting out in the sun to get a tan was ridiculous. In my nana's day a peachy white complexion was sought after. In fact, pictures of my nana in her heyday show her to have gorgeous clear, white, rosy skin. Old Box Brownie pictures of that era show people picnicking in the shade of leafy trees, big wide floppy hats, with no salacious skin showing, it was all long skirts and blouses.

Things have changed since those times. The depletion of the ozone layer has meant we are exposed to more UV rays than is healthy and we are happier to expose our skin.

I am one of those children of the '60s who sunbathed until I burned to achieve a dark tan. I remember lying on the silver roof of our carport and coating myself in vinegar and baby oil to get a great tan from the reflection off the roof. Being tanned was a great look and as my mother often said, 'A tan makes you look so healthy and much slimmer!'

It was hardly surprising when, at the age of 30, my doctor looked at a couple of moles on my leg and asked, 'How long have you had those?'

I had no idea.

They were both melanomas, one deeper than the other, and I had to have them cut out. I had a lucky near-miss, and from that day on I have never sunbathed or sat in the sun without some form of sunscreen or cover-up. I also think my skin is better for the years out of the sun. Initially I missed that sun-baked feeling you get after a day at the beach, that lovely warm glow which tingles all over. But I found if I covered up with saris and loose cotton kaftans I still got that feeling, just without the sunburn.

Studies are now beginning to show that our slip, slop, slapping has led to vitamin D deficiency. This is compounded by the fact that the very lotion we use to protect ourselves from cancer contains some of the nastiest chemicals around, which really shouldn't go anywhere near our skin. Especially not babies. No baby under six months should have sunscreen put anywhere near it. I'm not advocating a return to sun-baking but some sensible exposure to the sun is important for your health.

My Nana-natural attitude to sun is to avoid it during its strongest hours. I just don't go out on the beach between the hours of 11 am and 3 pm. Those are not the best times for gardening either so I usually just stay inside and work. If I do go out I cover up with loose shirts and long skirts and a good hat and sunglasses, and if I do need to use a sunscreen I use a natural product or one I make myself. There are many natural substances that will screen UV rays including sesame oil, black tea and zinc oxide cream. Natural sunscreens can be made without using chemical sun filters, artificial preservatives or synthetic colours. The problem is that most of the natural brands you buy give you a deathly white pallor as the cream acts as a physical barrier sitting on top of the skin rather than soaking into it. I just had to resign myself to the fact that I'd rather look like death than be dead.

I usually try to sit in the sun for at least 20 minutes a day, arms and legs uncovered, either side of the 11 am to 3 pm hot time to soak up some of that vital vitamin D.

By the end of summer I inevitably take on a golden colour because I spend a lot of time outdoors in the garden, walking or at the caravan, but I never get sunburned. My skin simply colours up naturally. And my regular skin checks, which I've had since my first moles were discovered 18 years ago, show no return of melanomas.

If you want to try my sunscreen recipe, it's on page 103. I love it because it leaves the skin supple and oiled at the end of the day, but be sensible and patch test it first. On my skin I think it has an SPF factor of about 15 but it will differ on other skin types. It should also be reapplied frequently, but I can't and won't offer any guarantees. Please use it at your own risk. This is safe for children but I also recommend using zinc oxide cream from the chemist. You'll remember in the '80s we used to put it on our noses in five fun fluoro colours. It is an excellent natural sunscreen for all children, especially babies, but I do encourage you not to rely solely on a sunscreen but opt for T-shirts and hats, big sun umbrellas and the shade of trees whenever your children are out in the sun.

By mid-January my radio shows have finished and we are ready for a few weeks at the caravan. I hate leaving the garden for so long as my tomatoes are laden with ripening fruit and need regular watering, my corn is easily the same height as me and growing fast, the cucumbers are nearly ready for picking, Lila's strawberries, which she feasts on every time she comes around, are producing full tilt and my salad greens will go to seed if we're not there to pick them regularly. And during the past few weeks I have been unable to resist the urge to use the garden centre vouchers I got from my mother-in-law for Christmas and cram even more plants into the garden.

I recently clipped a story out of the newspaper which listed the 12 foods most likely to contain pesticide residues in New Zealand. It went like this:
1. Celery
2. Peaches
3. Apricots
4. Butter/cream/cheese

5. Wheat, including bread
6. Apples
7. Plums
8. Mandarins
9. Raspberries
10. Oranges
11. Strawberries
12. Grapes/raisins/sultanas

I became determined to grow as many of these items as I could in my organic garden — and I was going to do it now.

In went the celery, which has proved to be a great plant to grow, because, like the salad greens you can take a stalk or two from the outside of it when you need it to make a salad and you don't need to buy half a plant, the bulk of which then wilts and rots in your fridge. Fresh celery also tastes gorgeously sweet and crisp, nothing like what you buy at the supermarket.

Peaches and apricots will have to wait until I have cleared down the side of our house to plant an urban orchard.

For the butter I found a recipe and presented Paul with a bottle of cream and the electric mixer.

'What are these for?' he asked.

'You are about to make butter,' I told him.

'You do it,' he said.

'I'm busy planting celery.'

He read the recipe and five minutes later was proudly holding up a big glob of butter.

'So easy!' he announced.

We added a bit of salt and sampled it.

'Delicious,' was all we could think to say.

We gathered up the buttermilk left over and made incredible scones with it for lunch. They were slathered with our home-made butter and some strawberry rose jam I had made the day before out of some leftover strawberries which were past their best.

'Yum!' said Pearl.

I was already making pumpernickel bread from organic rye and wheat, and where possible we bought organic bread so that was wheat taken care of.

Apples would also have to wait for the orchard.

We already had a plum tree planted out the front. Even though I had only got five precious fruit off the tree this year, I was sure it would do me proud next year. I had chosen the Hawera plum variety in honour of the New Zealand writer I love the most, Ronald Hugh Morrieson. He lived in Hawera and wrote such gorgeous books as *Came a Hot Friday, Scarecrow, Pallet on the Floor* and *Predicament*. I have first editions of all four of his books on my book shelf. Anything that comes from Hawera has to be good, I reasoned.

I also have a small but productive mandarin tree in the back garden, Lila's strawberries and a wonderful big Italian grape vine which first arrived here in New Zealand after World War II and grew in my garden from a clipping given to me by a friend. It was having its best year ever. So that just left oranges, Paul's favourite fruit, and raspberries, which we'd have to continue to buy, organic if we could find them.

Satisfied with our pesticide-free status I sent a group email to all the kids and asked them to organise a roster to feed and water the chickens and the gardens while we were away at the caravan. My niece Mariko, who loves to organise, volunteered to draw up a schedule and take charge of her four cousins, and we packed the car preparing to drive south safe in the knowledge that our family would mind the farm.

'Why have you filled the car with empty plastic bottles?' asked Paul as he was trying to squeeze in yet another box of books he was planning to get through at the caravan.

'Kaimai water,' was all I said.

'Yum, Kaimai water,' said Pearl in support.

'It's just water,' reasoned Paul. 'How do you even know it's safe to drink?'

'We don't,' said Pearl, 'but it tastes awesome.'

Not so long ago Pearl and I had been driving over the Kaimais and noticed that every time we passed a certain spot near the summit of the hill, cars were pulled over and people were filling bottles with water coming out of one of the rocky banks. We followed suit, filling up our drinking bottles with what turned out to be the freshest, coldest, best tasting water we had ever tried. I later found out that local Maori believe it has healing powers and that it comes to us from an aquifer which filters and aerates the water on its trip to the surface. Since then we never fail to stop and fill up as many empty bottles as we can find — much to Paul's horror.

'You know how much that stuff weighs?' he asked after I made him lug two 20-litre containers full of the stuff into the boot. 'Have you thought about your food miles here, the extra fossil fuels you are burning getting it all to Auckland?'

'Paul, we drive a Prius. It's a hybrid, it all works out in the end,' I said defensively, secretly realising that he had a point.

While my Prius cuts the cost of petrol by a third, and it has very low CO_2 emissions, adding the equivalent weight of a child to the car probably makes a bit of a difference. But I don't care. I love good water.

My quest for clean drinking water is apparently a little tiresome in my house. It started when we were living in Sydney during the lead-up to the 2000 Olympic Games. I came down with giardia and the only place I could have got it was the water. The doctor just shrugged and said 'Sydney water?

What are you going to do?'

Apparently giardia was quite common in Sydney's water supplies and I became convinced there was a cover-up because of the Olympics. I installed a water cooler at our house at great expense and never drank tap water. When we returned home to New Zealand I joined the army of people who bought bottled water, spending a fortune and creating mountains of empty plastic bottles. As my self-sufficiency leanings took over I opted instead for a filter jug, it isn't ideal but it's better than waking up in the morning to the smell of chlorine in your glass of water. If I want sparkling water, I just pop some filtered water in my SodaStream machine.

Paul, meanwhile, drinks from the tap with an attitude that no city council would let their citizens be poisoned and that treating the water with chlorine and fluoride is just sensible sanitation, not to mention great for kids' teeth.

I agree, my kids have had few fillings and have great teeth, which can be due to the fluoride in the water. But I don't agree with the whole population being dosed for some of the population and there must be a better way we can give fluoride to children who need it. Adding fluoride to water is now illegal in countries like Sweden, Switzerland and Holland. France, Austria and Belgium have never used it. And I just don't like the taste of chlorine. If I'm going to drink water for health I want it to be as good as I can get.

We have two 200-litre rainwater tanks installed on two of our downpipes, mainly for watering the garden, but when I can afford a steam distiller I'll be drinking purified rainwater.

We spend a blissful few weeks at the caravan, smoking mullet on our charcoal barbecue, eating crayfish given to us by our neighbour Maria. I cook pizza bread every night by popular request and we read, swim and kayak all day long.

We return to Auckland laden with bottles of Kaimai water, relaxed, well-read and Pearl and I have 'beach hair'. At the caravan we just let our hair go wild as a result of frequent swims and not too much attention in the brushing department.

Getting back to Auckland after a long time at the beach always reminds me of the Joni Mitchell song *Carey* which she wrote during her 'Blue' period where she escaped to join cave dwelling hippies in the caves of Crete, in Greece. She sings about having filthy fingernails, beach tar on her feet and missing her clean white linen and French cologne.

We walk down the long hallway of our old villa and marvel at how big our house is after living in a space the size of our bathroom for two weeks. I always head straight out the back to check on the chickens who seem very well looked after and content, and to survey my garden which is laden with produce, ready to be harvested. The cats come to greet us, swirling around our legs and meowing for some attention.

Pearl will be back at school in a few days, and the real world beckons. A world of deadlines for Paul and I as we launch back into our writing and attempt to earn back some of the money we have just paid out to the tax department as we do every year on 15 January. Despite that, it's nice to be back into the swing of things, cooking in our rumpty old kitchen and sleeping in our big bed.

Cleaning Paste

1 cup baking soda

1 tablespoon cream of tartar

10 ml liquid castile soap

3 ml water

1 ml peppermint essential oil

In a bowl, mix together the baking soda with the cream of tartar. In a jug mix liquid castile soap and the water. Slowly pour into the powders and mix with a fork until you have a paste. Add more water if you need to. Add peppermint essential oil and stir to combine. Store in an airtight container and use to clean kitchen and bathroom sinks, baths and toilets.

Laundry Clay/Powder

Depending on your ingredients this may turn out to be a powder or a clay, both work just as well.

1 cup washing soda

1 cup baking soda

60 ml liquid castile soap

2 ml lavender essential oil

Put the washing soda in a food processor and reduce the lumpy crystals as much as you can. Slowly drizzle in the liquid castile soap while the processor is still running to create a white frothy paste. Then add the baking soda and the lavender oil and continue to process until you have something resembling white clay. Keep it in an airtight container and use a tablespoon for an average load, double if you are washing a big load.

Cottage Cheese

The hardest thing about this recipe is finding the rennet, called Renco at your supermarket. They usually keep it by the custard powder but you will probably have to ask for it. This cheese will last in the fridge for about a week and I keep mine in a beetroot keeper – one of those plastic storage jars with a basket inside which you lift out.

3 tablespoons skim milk powder

600 ml full-fat milk

1 teaspoon Renco rennet

Mix a little milk with the milk powder to form a paste in the bottom of a saucepan and then add the rest of the milk. Heat to lukewarm, no hotter. Add the rennet and stir. Set aside in a warm place for 15 minutes to set. Get a carving knife or similar and cut the curds by slicing it in a grid pattern to get lots of little centimetre wide squares (this releases the whey). Line a sieve with a paper kitchen towel or muslin and pour the mixture into it. Leave over a bowl to drain for about two hours, or longer if you like it drier. Mash up with a fork if it needs it and store in the fridge. Feed the drained liquid to your dog — mine loves it!

Ricotta

You don't need rennet for this, just a few lemons off the tree. Make sure you use really good whole fat milk. This can be a bit tricky as you don't want to heat it so hot that the curds don't form but you will need to simmer on a gentle heat for a while, so be patient. This cheese will keep for a week and is absolutely delicious with lemon curd on sourdough toast!

2 litres full fat milk

1 cup cream

3 tablespoon freshly squeezed lemon juice

½ teaspoon salt

Put the milk and cream in a good, heavy-based saucepan or preserving pan and heat slowly until it is just on the boil. Add the lemon juice and salt and reduce the heat to allow it to simmer. After about five minutes you should see the curds separate from the whey, if not turn the heat up a little but do not let boil! Once you see the separation take place, take the pot off the heat and gently pour the mixture into a sieve which you have lined with muslin, cheesecloth, a fine weave tea-towel or a clean lace curtain.

Gather up the cloth and tie at the top then hang from your tap or over the bath to drain for 15 minutes. Let cool and then keep in the fridge. I use the beetroot keeper to hold the ricotta and allow it to drain.

Pizza Bread

This is a family favourite adapted from a recipe Alison Gofton gave me years ago.

2 teaspoons active granulated yeast (not Surebake)

½ teaspoon sugar

1½ cups of warm water

4 large cups of high grade flour ('Tipo 00' Italian pizza flour if possible)

salt and pepper

1 cup of chopped basil or parsley (optional)

4 tablespoons olive oil

extra flour (if required)

Put yeast and sugar into warm water and mix together. Set aside in a warm place. Sift flour with salt and pepper into a bowl and add basil or parsley if you like. It is just as good without the herbs. When the yeast mixture starts to froth — and only when it froths — mix in olive oil. Add the yeast mixture to the flour and

mix to dough. Add more flour if it's a little sticky.
Don't knead. Put in bowl in warm place and leave to
rise for about an hour or until double the size. (If you
can't find a warm place for the dough to rise, which
can be hard in winter, simply fill a hot-water bottle
and sit the bowl on that.) Pat out into breads and
barbecue or fry. Brush with olive oil and sprinkle with
lots of sea salt.

Butter

salt, to taste

600 ml cream

Simply pour the cream in a bowl, get out your electric
beaters and whisk until lumps of butter appear and
eventually form a big lump. It takes about five minutes
on a medium speed. Remove the lump of butter and
douse it in a bowl of cold water squeezing gently. Rinse
under a running tap and then put in a bowl and use.
Add salt to taste.

Strawberry Rose Jam

You can adjust this recipe to use up a punnet of
strawberries that doesn't get eaten. Instead of letting
it go to waste, whip up a jar full of jam. I often
make single jars of jam at the caravan using leftover
strawberries or the blackberries that grow wild there.
If you are new to jam making, you can make life a lot
easier by buying a sugar which has added pectin in it

to ensure a good set. I put lemon in this recipe as its natural pectin helps it to set. But if your jam doesn't set, you can always call it a conserve.

500 grams fresh strawberries, hulled

350 grams sugar

zest and juice of half a lemon

1 tablespoon rosewater

Mash up the strawberries a little, not too much, just so that there is a good mix of pulp and lumps of fruit. Stir in the remaining ingredients and heat on the stove gently until the sugar is dissolved. Turn up the heat so that it bubbles and keep it on the boil for about 10–15 minutes until it thickens. To test if it is ready take a teaspoonful and drop it onto a plate. It should form a wrinkly skin and when you pull your finger through the middle of the blob it should leave a channel in the liquid, not fill up again. While hot pour into your sterilised jar and seal. (See page 141 for preserving tips.)

Sunscreen

75 ml sesame oil

45 grams coconut oil or cocoa butter

15 grams beeswax

120 ml water

2 tablespoons zinc oxide (from chemist)

1 tablespoon wheat germ oil

1 teaspoon citric acid (from supermarket baking aisle)

20 drops lavender oil

In a double boiler (or put a bowl over boiling water in a saucepan) melt the oils and the beeswax together. Take off the heat and add the water, mixing with an electric mixer until thick and creamy. Then add the zinc oxide, wheat germ oil, and citric acid. Stir then add the lavender oil. Over time this will start leaching water — just drain it off

FEBRUARY

his month turns out to be, once again, dominated by the hens. While we get back into the routine of school and deadlines, we have a new addition to the family, called Matilda.

She was found hiding under a trailer at the campground. Newly-hatched, a black fluffy chick, she was held up to me in a little box and the next thing I knew she was mine. I gave no thought to the two years it had taken for me to persuade Paul to agree to us getting three chickens, I just knew instinctively that he wouldn't mind a fourth. And I was right.

Initially she was named Chanel by fashion-conscious Pearl, then Blanche after our favourite character on *Coronation Street*, and finally Paul named her Matilda because she hatched on Australia Day. What I didn't realise was that adopting a day-old chick meant more than just keeping her in a box and throwing some food in. She screeched constantly, she had to be taught how to eat, how to drink, hot-water bottles were needed night and day and the only place she was truly happy was snuggled into my neck where she liked to poo . . . frequently.

By day three I resorted to putting her in the car so that we could have a little peace in our caravan for an afternoon nap.

'Sick of her already?' asked the woman in the next caravan.

'Not sick of her, just need a break,' I replied full of guilt, tripping over myself with exhaustion. 'It's as bad as having a new baby.'

'Did you put them in the car as well?' she inquired before giving a bit of advice: 'You don't want her to cook in there.'

'It's a Prius,' I said rather smugly. 'It has a solar panel in the roof that operates a fan which keeps the temperature in the car at just the right heat for a tiny chick!'

I stomped off safe in the knowledge that the temperature was automatically controlled.

Then we had to bring her home to Auckland. Pearl sat grim-faced as Matilda — in a cardboard box at her feet — screeched all the way home.

'How does one introduce a baby chick to three established hens?' I Googled, I emailed, I posted on Twitter and Facebook, expecting the usual straightforward replies such queries have always received.

Turns out one doesn't. Horror stories came flooding in of baby chicks being pecked to death. Apparently they start at their bottom and the sight of blood sparks a frenzy of pecking. The worst story came from someone who thought she had successfully integrated her new chick: all went well for three days and then the chick was found dead. The storyteller advised getting another chick for safety in numbers.

'We don't even know if Matilda is a Matilda,' said Paul, quite correctly pointing out that she may be a rooster. 'The last thing we need is another chick who might turn out to be a rooster as well.'

Back to the computer. 'How do you tell if your chick is male or female?' I Googled.

Turns out you can't.

'We'll hire a chicken sexer,' said Paul who thought they might be listed in the Yellow Pages.

'Oh great, so you're going to drive out to Tegel or wherever they work and thrust Matilda at them in their tea break?'

I then pointed out that the sexer can only tell the difference if the chicken is a day old.

'We'll just have to wait and see if she starts crowing,' I said,

'How long will that take?' he asked reasonably.

'About five months. But apparently some roosters never crow,' I said. 'And some people in cities bring them inside at night and put them in the bathroom covered up to keep the light out so they don't know to crow.'

'Not us,' is all he said.

Meanwhile Matilda made my office her home. And in an effort to get the other hens used to her being around I put her in the coop when the others come out in the morning, safely locked up but able to run around and have frequent dust baths (more proof in my eyes that she is indeed a hen.) Then, at the end of the day, she comes back inside for the night when they go to bed.

'I think I'll do supervised visits with Marigold, Hillary

and Yoko,' I proposed. 'Surely that will work.'

I fell in love all over again with Matilda as her feathers grew in. I marvelled at her black and white plumage and was secretly chuffed that whenever I sat anywhere near her she would run over to me and she was never happier than when she was perched on some part of my body, grooming herself and me. As she grew she began to resemble a bald eagle, prompting a momentary panic from myself, wondering if perhaps that little chick found under the trailer was actually a hawk, and then comforting myself by going online and seeing similar pictures of geeky, weird looking eight-week-old chicks.

I did pause to wonder why I had taken on yet another animal needing my attention when I was already fairly busy with the other seven. Then one fine Saturday afternoon all hell broke loose.

'Do we have any KY jelly?'

It's a question I don't usually ask Paul on a Saturday afternoon, but he was in an awkward position.

He was holding our hen Hillary backwards and I was peering at her back-end. She was in a bit of trouble. Actually I'll re-phrase that. Her insides where coming out of her bottom. I think, in midwife terms, that is what you call a prolapsed uterus. She was also eggbound, which I think, in midwife terms, is what you would call, 'can't push the bloody thing out'.

We were officially having an animal emergency and my usual source of poultry-keeping wisdom, the internet, advised a delicate rubbing of KY Jelly.

When we first got our hens we made the decision, rather wisely, that if one of them got into a bit of trouble we would not call a vet. They only cost us $20 each so why would we pay $1000 – our last vet bill for an animal emergency – to get them fixed up? Better to do like the farmers do and have a cull.

I gloved up, and tentatively rubbed Hillary's bottom, technically called a vent, with sex lubricant thinking rather ridiculously that olive oil might have been a greener option.

'Oh God, this is so disgusting,' I managed to screech before Paul yelled: 'We're losing her,' in his serious voice. The one Dr McDreamy uses on *Grey's Anatomy*.

Hillary's head was hanging low, her eyes were closed. She looked just like a dead chicken you see hanging in Asian markets overseas.

I rang the vet. He wasn't in. I scribbled down the emergency number. I dialled.

'Phlopp,' said Hillary's bottom.

An egg sped past my leg and landed triumphantly onto the kitchen floor, smashing and spreading in all its yolky glory.

The KY had done the trick. Or Paul had squeezed her in his panic. We'll never know.

We put her back outside and played TV doctors and nurses with high-fives and modest 'it was nothing really' letting the adrenalin wash over us in a post-emergency high.

I looked out the back. Hillary's eyes were closing again, she was straining, she was not looking good.

'We're losing her! Again!' I shouted in my television nurse voice.

'Look what's hanging out of her, now,' said Paul as he reluctantly picked her up and pointed her bottom in my direction for round two.

I gloved up, I gathered what was hanging and attempted to shove it all back in, closing one eye and squinting through the other, as if somehow that would make the whole nauseating experience more palatable to my retina.

'Phlopp.'

Out popped another egg, narrowly missing my ear before landing on the deck.

I gathered and poked what was hanging out back where I presumed it belonged, then doused it all down with warm salt water.

'I think I'm going to throw up,' I muttered as I collapsed into the deck chair. Wrung out like a television surgeon after an all night brain operation.

'It wasn't really that bad,' ventured Paul, who to this day claims it was his gentle squeezing that snatched Hillary back from the jaws of death.

'You've obviously never been in labour,' I snapped back. 'My uterus is in turmoil.'

Meanwhile Hillary had returned to the garden where she sat down for a second, had a think and then popped up to resume her normal activities of terrorising the cats and ripping the soil to shreds.

'Isn't she marvellous,' Paul chuckled like a new father freshly emerged from the delivery room.

I made a cup of tea with a teaspoon of sugar for the shock and kept a close eye on Hillary. I guess I hoped she might give me a thank-you peck, or I might catch a soft, grateful look in her beady eyes rather like the lion who had the thorn removed from his paw by Androcles.

None was forthcoming.

Paul bustled around cleaning up the eggs and the two pairs of discarded gloves. He held up the KY Jelly cautiously between two fingers.

'I told you that would come in useful one day.'

Hillary has since had a couple of other egg-bound episodes but none as dramatic as this and I've even had a vet congratulate us on our deft handling of the potentially life threatening situation. I've also resumed dosing the hens with a teaspoon of colloidal silver in their water to help fight any infections, which might have been what caused Hillary to bind. I also added linseed to their diet to help out with omega-3 and skin elasticity, especially in the vent area. Apparently this is also good for us, as the eggs will now have more omega-3 content than before.

Hillary's egg binding took me about a week to get over and it very nearly sent me back on the booze.

With all the hen action we barely had time to register the fact that we had decided to give up drinking for the month of February. It is something I had been meaning to do for years, mainly to prove to myself that I could. I'm no longer a heavy drinker but I like a glass of wine or two a night, which all my research tells me is quite healthy – better little and often than a binge. But niggling in the back of my mind was the fact that I seemed to structure my day around that first drink, it was a signal that my work day had finished and it was time to start cooking dinner and relaxing with the family.

When you work from home it becomes very important to have these signals because it is very easy to let work slip over into family time and before you know it you are still tapping away at the keyboard at 7 pm, there's no dinner on the table and everyone's grumpy. We have a rule that our computers get shut down by 6 pm at the latest, unless someone is on a terror deadline and needs to work through. So, at 5.30 pm, out comes the wine, I sift through my emails to check I've replied to everyone I need to, check on my Twitter and Facebook pages, update my website and then clock off. This month, I just needed to prove to myself that I could still function without that lovely crisp glass of white in my hand.

Pearl helpfully pointed out that I had stopped for three years once before.

I looked at her blankly. Three days without a drink, maybe, but never three Christmases, three birthdays and three wedding anniversaries.

'No darling, I think you must have me mistaken for that other mother, the one who goes to church on Sundays and irons your school uniform every morning at six.'

'Yes you did. Four pregnancies. Four times nine months equals three years,' she said slowly, as if dealing with a small child unfamiliar with the concept of mathematics or the gestation period of a human.

'Of course, I hadn't thought about that,' I said gratefully. 'And actually all of you were overdue so it was more like 10 months so that's nearly three and a half years.'

With that I marched off feeling confident about my impending 28 days of sobriety. So confident that I began early – on 31 January.

I knew that to change any pattern of behaviour you need to identify the triggers that encourage the behaviour. By day two I had identified all 20 of them and realised with horror that the first trigger appeared at 10 am. Not that I have ever had a drink at 10 am, I just start thinking about what I would have to drink after work. Sauvignon blanc or chardonnay? Rosé or pinot noir? Or is it a martini type of day?

As the triggers piled on top of each other throughout the day like drunken university students squashing themselves into a Mini, the major trigger or Big Daddy, as I came to call it, would appear at 5.30 pm on the dot and start jumping up and down on the Mini causing all the other triggers to squeal with delight.

'What you need is a nice exotic drink to look forward to sampling at the end of every day,' suggested Pearl. 'Let's go to the Asian.'

'The Asian' is not a wise old wizened up man who

112

survived Pol Pot and ekes out a living dispensing exotic drinks. It is the local Asian supermarket where there is a shelf as long as a football field laden with pink, green, purple and orange drinks full of things like coconut jelly, sago and lychees.

We filled a trolley with two of each. After three days I attempted to look at the labels to see what I was actually ingesting and found myself lacking the language skills to complete the task. Lurking in the back of my mind was a mini version of the melamine poisoning of baby's milk in China and so I gave up on the exotic drinks, preferring instead to invent my own.

By day 12 I was living on my sun tea and keeping the Big Daddy-trigger happy in the evenings with my virgin version of a Turkish Gin because as it turns out, he was quite happy with a hit of sugar instead of the alcohol.

What I hadn't prepared for was the other Big Daddy trigger, Paul, who had joined me on my alcohol-free month. He planted himself in my office at the end of a particularly stressful day and suggested that we both go 'off plan' and have a night on the booze.

'No way,' I said resolutely.

I put it out to my social networking friends on Facebook and Twitter who I had been spending more time with lately due to the lack of drinking.

'You decide. At 5.30 pm I'll add up your votes,' I posted.

By 5.30 pm all the women said keep it up and the men said have a drink you silly old trout. I was not at all surprised and buoyed by my social network sisterhood I was determined to keep going.

At that moment Paul appeared in my office clutching two glass flutes and a bottle of chilled champagne, the bottle beaded with dew.

Our daughter looked at us with horror.

'I'm so disillusioned,' she said sullenly.

'Never mind,' I chuckled letting the delicious bubbles cascade down my parched throat. 'Life is full of disappointments.'

I had learned a valuable lesson during my almost-month of sobriety. When your hen nearly dies and you've just stuck your hand up her bum not once but twice, instead of turning to the whisky to treat the shock, grab a towel and head to the nearest beach for a swim. And when your friends ask you to lunch, delay it for a month because no matter how many times they say 'I promise I won't pressure you to have a wine,' they will. And at 5.30 pm instead of reaching for a glass of wine, hire a treadmill and get on that for a half-hour run instead.

The treadmill, which now lives downstairs, was one of the best ideas for fitness I've ever had. Except it wasn't my idea. Inspired by my mate Kerre Woodham's book, *Short Fat Chick to Marathon Runner*, I started running about two years ago. After years of joining gyms then not going or putting myself on strict walking routines or joining fitness classes and losing interest, I followed the plan for beginners as set out by her trainer, Gareth Brown. Before too long I was running 10 minutes without stopping, then 30 and then on one Sunday afternoon I ran for a whole hour along the waterfront. Even if the last 20 minutes were spent hobbling because my left knee was protesting loudly, I was determined to complete my goal of being able to run for an hour.

What I did by 'running through the pain' was damage my knee. It took a year to fix that, and then when I started running again my hip screamed at me. After physio sessions and cycling at the gym I basically gave up on exercise because it hurt.

'All exercise hurts at some stage,' reasoned Paul who

works out at the gym most days.

'Not this hurt. Not "old lady, can't get out of bed, can't walk down the hall" hurt. The only way to stop it hurting is to not exercise, so I am going to "listen to my body".'

'Your choice,' he mumbled. 'If she says "listen to my body" one more time!' I heard him whisper to himself.

It is true, a lot of the way I live involves having a listen to my body — and odds are by the time you finish this book you will be sick of me saying that too!

Finally Kerre recommended a chiropractor and off I went. An X-ray revealed that my childbearing hips, which had carried and delivered four 10-pound babies, were out of kilter. Not just lopsided but tilted the wrong way as well. After several weeks of clicking and crunching to get my spine aligned, they had come right. A lot of people find the clicking and crunching off-putting, but I love a good session on the chiropractor's couch. Initially I would leave feeling totally alien in my body as it slowly adjusted to having the correct posture.

Finally I was pronounced straight and my spine in full working order and that moment coincided with a long, lovely lunch with the woman I now credit with my fitness, the aforementioned Kerre. She had invited a few friends for her birthday and after a few wines I started talking to a nice man whose face I vaguely recognised from the media. 'Something to do with rugby,' I thought to myself and that's as far as I got as my interest in rugby came to a grinding halt when I was 15 and broke up with my boyfriend who was a prop in the first XV.

'You sound like you know a bit about fitness,' I jumped in to the conversation.

'Yes, a bit,' he said modestly.

I then proceeded to pour out my woes from sore knee to hip to chiropractor.

'What you need to do,' he said very kindly, 'is hire a treadmill, just for three months and then build up your running programme again very slowly. You'll find that the treadmill is a lot softer than hard ground so you won't get the shuddering on your body that you would if you ran outside.'

He then spent another 10 minutes giving me a training programme which I have stuck to, including hiring a treadmill. 'Wow, that guy has been so helpful with my running,' I commented to Paul. 'He's really inspired me to get back into it. Is he a fitness trainer do you think?'

Paul could barely contain his mirth. 'Wendyl, you have just spent the last 15 minutes getting one-to-one fitness advice from the former All Black coach John Hart.'

'Oh gosh,' I was mortified.

I now walk 30 minutes a day, pain-free as long as I remember to do my stretches and keep my spine clicked and do yoga once a week. Exercise is a very good alternative for that half hour between 5.30 and 6 when I would otherwise be winding down with a few wines. Although − truth be told − I often have a wine afterwards.

One night during our dry February when Paul and I found it impossible not to have a wee tipple was Valentine's night. We have always made a bit of a fuss of this night, not so much with big fancy presents, but always a gorgeous meal that, if possible, will always include his chocolate mousse. The first meal Paul ever cooked for me had this mousse as dessert and as the saying goes 'He had me at the mousse'. It is a lovely bitter orangey mousse which doesn't leave you feeling ill from the richness of it. Just completely happy and satiated.

We also make sure we spend a few hours together acknowledging the gift that a good relationship can be, but also the hard work that goes into it. Our relationship like most has needed some fine tuning and a lot of patience on both sides, but as Paul always says the main reason it works is because we disagree on the unimportant things and agree on the important ones.

Our letterbox is a case in point.

It all started when my mother-in-law turned up on the doorstep out of breath.

'I was going to drop these off in the letterbox but there doesn't appear to be any bottom in it,' she announced taking long lung-filling gasps of air every three words.

It's quite an effort to get to our front door involving a steep path, steps and a fair bit of fauna and flora clearing.

A cup of coffee and a sit down saw to my mother-in-law, but alas the letterbox on closer inspection, just like Hillary, did indeed have no bottom. Suddenly the fact that our mail was being delicately slipped under the locked door of our garage, five metres to the right of the letterbox, made sense. We just thought our mailman had gone a little odd and preferred the slot under the door than the slot in the box. We also understood why we frequently had to hunt in our overgrown garden looking for our mail.

Our letterbox was old when we moved in. It was possibly constructed at the same time as the garage, which is pre-1940s. And like the garage, which is barely standing, we just didn't want to see that our letterbox was past it. We were convinced it was made from heart kauri and was so old and iconic we considered registering it as a historic place.

My mother-in-law offered to buy Paul a new one for his birthday but he couldn't wait that long. Instead he instructed me to have a look on TradeMe, and a week later our marriage was severely strained. Who knew that men and women could think so differently about a letterbox?

'Not white, not metal, slot needs to be wider, too big,

honestly how do you think that is going to fit on our post?' he barked as I showed him my TradeMe selection of iconic and slightly weathered Kiwiana letterboxes.

'Put in a search for "letterbox wooden",' he instructed — again — before marching off to address some literary crisis on librarything.com.

Unused to being instructed, let alone twice in one morning, I went for a long walk to consider my options. Would I tear his heart out now or give him another 24 hours? As I walked I felt the same way I did when I got pregnant. Overnight you notice every pram, every baby, every other pregnant woman and that whole aisle in the supermarket with nappies in it when, the day before, they simply didn't register on your radar. I stopped and admired every single letterbox, from the architect-designed cedar and metal creations currently in vogue for Grey Lynn renovators, to various versions of the nice white metal one with room for four bottles of milk in a carrier I remembered from my childhood, to the quirky artistic creations ranging from one painted to look like a TV and another involving pukeko and a great deal of ceramics. In Grey Lynn when people aren't appearing on or making television, they express themselves with artistic letterboxes.

I returned home more confused than ever and stroked my broken letterbox. I'd never had to replace a letterbox before and you certainly don't know what you've got till it's gone. Perhaps I could patch it, but where would I find the right grade and age of heart kauri to match?

'I need to talk to you about the letterbox,' I said to Paul in the voice I use for getting my own way. 'You're being bossy and unreasonable and I really want one of those white metal ones from my childhood.'

'I was not bossy,' he retorted. 'I just thought you'd appreciate my input.'

'Next you'll be blaming the full moon and the hot summer,' I snarled, instantly regretting it.

'Right, I can see there's only one way to sort this, get in the car we're going to Mitre 10,' he instructed — again.

The good news is that we now have another letterbox, even though we left a trail of helpful Mitre 10 staff in our wake as they all tried to calm the war of the worlds taking place in the letterbox aisle, before sensibly retreating to the safety of the lawnmower section.

Our new letterbox is a wooden version of the white one and if you squint your eyes you could almost call it iconic.

'Happy now?' Paul grumped, content only that he got to choose the number to put on it, which is quite frankly gaudy.

By Valentine's Day all memory of the letterbox incident has been erased and I decided to develop a romance pillow spray, which I made up and gave to all my friends. There's just something about preparing for a night of romance that I think all women enjoy because we are more into environment and intimacy than most men. I made the spray up out of rosewater, ylang ylang, bergamot and jasmine and it gives off the most heady, relaxing smell. Ylang ylang is well known as an essential oil to encourage romance and jasmine and bergamot go well with it. I send it out to friends and get encouraging reports back.

Most evenings in February are spent in the garden harvesting. It is best to harvest your produce at the end of the day when the nutrients are at their strongest so I do the rounds of tomatoes, corn, salad greens, cucumber, beetroot, beans, capsicums, chillis and herbs for dinner. I combine the tomatoes and basil with avocado for quick salads, or make a salsa out of the tomatoes, corn, cucumber and chilli. I grate fresh beetroot with fresh carrot for a sweet, raw salad and sprinkle it with lemon juice and a little oil. The beans we eat raw or just lightly steamed.

At this stage the garden is producing just enough for us to eat and no more. Later I will be utterly sick of the vast amounts of produce coming in from the garden, but in February it is just right and it is the first month of the year where we eat mostly our own produce.

We are often found of a Friday night enjoying the warm weather outside with friends. One night some friends came for a drink and we invited them to stay. I felt like a female Hugh Fearnley Whittingstall from the River Cottage television shows as I popped in and out of the garden grabbing bits and pieces for dinner. I had long ago stopped holding up my produce for everyone to see, incredibly proud of myself, and opted to simply trot past back to the kitchen with my haul.

'Are you cooking from your garden?' asked one of our friends enthusiastically.

'It's nothing really' I said, suddenly shy about the fact that after years of learning how to garden I had achieved my dream of cooking a meal from scratch for friends from my produce.

'You're amazing' he said, meaning it.

'Thank you,' I said, meaning it.

I made a quinoa salad using all our produce combined with some free-range chicken breasts we had in the fridge. We feasted on grapes from our vine for dessert along with some ginger crunch Paul had made a few weeks ago and thrown in the freezer. I like to encourage people to try newly available, but very old grains and in the case of quinoa (pronounced keen-wa) it is full of good stuff. It is high in protein and calcium and is also a good source of iron, phosphorous, B vitamins and vitamin E. The Incas called it the 'mother grain' and it is a nice, faster cooking alternative to brown rice with a sweet, nutty taste.

We discovered it after we both decided to go on the Sonoma Diet, an eating plan that concentrates on ten power foods: whole grains, almonds, capsicums, tomatoes, broccoli, grapes, spinach, blueberries, strawberries and olive oil. It uses many ancient grains and lets you drink wine after week one, which is why we chose it.

We learned a lot about the power of grains, but also a sage lesson on why Paul should never diet. After the first week he came into my office.

'I can't see,' he announced as he stumbled in doing a very good impression of a blind man.

'Nonsense,' I replied engrossed in a piece I was writing.

Ten minutes later he returned.

'Seriously I can't see,' he tried again.

'Why is it that whenever I need to write you crash in here with some tale of woe?' I grumbled refusing to look away from my computer screen as my story approached the finish line.

Five minutes later he returned.

'Can you at least have a look at my glasses?' he pleaded. 'Maybe they're broken and that's why I can't see.'

It wasn't the glasses. It was the diet. A week into our new diet and Paul was a blind man.

Fortunately I am the daughter of a diabetic and was able to diagnose a symptom of low blood-sugar on the spot and administer high doses of bananas, barley sugars and fruit juice.

Paul meanwhile wandered around the house alternating between banging into walls and looking dazed and confused.

'How could this have happened?' he wondered out loud.

'A few words spring to mind such as "dogged" "determined" and "bloody stupid,"' I responded.

Paul had launched into his first ever diet with evangelical enthusiasm which combined with his annoying habit of following the letter to the law and exercising for two hours a day meant that by my calculation he was living on about 800 calories a day. And all this for a big man who should probably take in about 3000 calories just to function correctly.

'You need to lighten up on yourself,' I had commented the day before he lost his sight. He had run into an old friend who was setting up a baking stall and had made him a gift of a very plump ginger kiss.

'I palmed it,' he told me. 'I can't be eating that stuff, it's pure sugar.'

'Everyone on a diet cheats, it's just a ginger kiss,' I reasoned.

'Nonsense. Why would you go on a diet and not follow it exactly?' he replied, puffed up with rectitude.

It took about five hours for his sight to return to normal. I watched him like a hawk, only too aware that at any moment he could keel over in a coma. But the drama of losing his eyesight wasn't enough to say goodbye to the diet.

'I'll just add a fruit serving,' announced the manorexic-in-training.

The next day he lost an entire story he had been working on for two days, forgetting to save to his hard drive as he was writing. I thought he was going to cry, then he went to bed at II o'clock in the morning. I kept nudging him awake and asking him what day of the week it was and who our prime minister was. Then I went to the wine shop.

'Get this down you and then you're having a proper meal,' I instructed.

'Are you drinking again?' Pearl asked eyeing up the wine glasses.

'Yeah, Daddy needs the sugar,' I reasoned.

'Oh thank goodness for that,' she said. 'You guys have been so weird all week.'

One bottle became two.

Later that evening our daughter entered the lounge to find her parents behaving entirely normally for the first time that week. Her father was blissfully asleep sitting upright on the couch, and her mother was sobbing her eyes out because Juno had just given her baby away in the movie.

'Bedtime!' she informed us before switching off the TV and putting the dog out. 'I'm so glad you two are back.'

It takes half an hour to make the quinoa salad, the exact amount of time it takes to get a pizza delivered which used to be – and sometimes still is – our default Friday night meal when friends pop in. We have traded a highly processed combination of white flour, sugars, cheese and fatty meats for a whole grain meal full of nutrients.

I have to stop myself giving our guests my lecture about how I only eat foods my grandmother would recognise, when I realise Nana would probably never have heard of quinoa. And besides Paul has told me I'm becoming a bit of a nutrition bore.

'It's great that you are finding out so much about healing the body through nutrition and ridding ourselves of highly processed foods, but sometimes people just want to sit down and enjoy a meal for what it is. Good food, cooked well and eaten with friends. So shut the hell up!'

I took his point. But it doesn't stop me reading and compiling information for what I like to call my Nana diet which is slowly influencing the way I cook and eat and will eventually become a personal challenge. It's okay to be a nana but can you eat like one too?

Romance Pillow Spray

80 ml water

20 ml rosewater

1 teaspoon vodka

2 drops ylang ylang essential oil

1 drop bergamot essential oil

1 drop jasmine essential oil

Add all the ingredients together in a glass jug and whisk together with a kitchen whisk. The vodka is to help the oils disperse in the liquid. Pour into a spray bottle and enjoy.

Pure jasmine oil is very expensive but please invest in just 2 ml as you will use it time and time again. If it is diluted in another oil it won't have the same effect.

Quinoa Salad

1 cup quinoa

4 chicken breasts

1 onion

1 capsicum

2 ears of fresh corn

1 cup mushrooms

2 cups chicken stock

4 tablespoons olive oil

Juice of 1 lemon

handful parsley or basil, finely chopped

Rinse quinoa well to remove the bitter outer coating
then put in a pot with the stock, bring to the boil
and simmer for 15 minutes, or until all the liquid is
absorbed. Meanwhile poach chicken breasts and fry up
onion, capsicum, corn and mushrooms.

To create salad, squeeze the juice of a small lemon
into a big bowl and whisk in the olive oil. Throw in
quinoa with the vegetables and sliced chicken. Sprinkle
through the finely chopped fresh parsley or basil and
serve.

Sun Tea

4 herbal tea bags (I use green tea and berry)

1 litre water

Find a glass jar (not plastic as it may leach chemicals
in the sun). Place four fruity teabags into the jar. I use
a blend of green tea and berries, or you can just go
straight for a berry mix – they need to be very fruity.
Pour on water and then sit it in the hot sun. It will
gradually take on a bright pink colour and the tea will
have steeped. Bring inside, store in the fridge and serve
over lots of ice and a slice of lemon. If you have a sweet
tooth, add some sugar or stevia.

Paul's Chocolate Mousse

300 ml cream

200 grams dark chocolate

4 cups brown sugar

4 egg yolks

1 tablespoon Grand Marnier

1 teaspoon vanilla

2 teaspoons grated orange rind

60 grams unsalted butter

Heat cream until bubbles form around edges. Do
not boil. Place chopped chocolate, sugar, egg yolks,
Grand Marnier, rind and vanilla in a blender. Pour
in hot cream while blending on high speed for about a
minute. Drop butter in 1 tsp at a time while you blend.
Continue to blend until smooth. Pour into eight
serving glasses. Refrigerate 1 to 2 hours before serving.

MARCH

By the time March rolls around I am usually fairly grumpy with my garden. It is the one month of the year when I look at it and just can't be bothered anymore. It's like the end of a love affair that started in the spring full of hope and expectation, wore itself out over summer and is now just hanging around making a nuisance of itself. Usually the plants are exhausted from their crop, the soil is drying up and the bugs have taken over. I don't see any point in wasting water on plants and I am usually at my busiest with work, so we have a standoff for about a week where tomatoes rot on the ground, corn gets massacred by bugs and the only thing standing tall and strong are the chillies, which seem to thrive on neglect.

After a week of ignoring the garden, I get out there with Paul and some buckets and we harvest everything off the plants while the older hens run around our feet whooping for joy. Matilda is still too little to enjoy this March treat. They love nothing better than being part of any gardening expedition as it usually reveals a supply of bugs falling off the plants or worms and bugs revealed when we dig. We take our harvest inside and spend a weekend bottling up the tomatoes and freezing anything else.

I repeat my favourite Arabiatta recipe simply because it is still the easiest and most reliable way to store tomatoes into the winter and never fails to reward you when you bring it out, heat it up and throw it on your pasta. This month I've started putting together a great pasta dish I altered from a Nigel Slater recipe which takes just half an hour from vine to table.

Then, if I really can't be bothered, I just bundle up the tomatoes, put them in plastic bags and throw them into the freezer. In the winter they will make welcome additions to stews and curries. If there's any basil left over it goes into the food processor with a little oil and is mulched up and poured into ice cube trays to be frozen before I put the the frozen cubes into plastic bags to store in the freezer. Any corn we can't eat goes straight over the fence to the hens who cannot get enough of it. I figure we get the nutrition back in the gorgeous yellow egg yolks they produce as a result of it. We always grab a few bunches of oregano, which self seeds and grows all over my garden every summer. We put them upside down in a brown paper bag on top of the fridge (or in the hot-water cupboard, if you have one). A month later we sit at the kitchen table with a glass of wine and pull all the dry leaves off, before putting them in jars. They are then destined to be crumbled on Paul's famous cheese on toast, and of course, into pasta sauces or pizzas. Paul says the oregano is the best complement for melted cheese you can find.

Once all that is done, I let the hens out onto the now

depleted garden for a week. They are my clean-up crew and it takes them the whole week to go over all the garden beds, digging and scratching and leaving the soil nicely turned over and aerated. Then I fertilise the garden with horse manure, which I buy at the gate of a house on the road near Matamata on my way back from the caravan. The hens go wild looking for any grubs or larvae in there and once again spread it all out and dig it into my garden.

I am finding that the hens are efficient cleaners for a lot of things. One morning I get up early and discover to my horror that there are maggots all over the kitchen floor. They seem to be wriggling themselves out from under the fridge, where something has obviously rolled and proceeded to rot over the summer without us knowing. I have the brilliant idea of bringing the hens into the kitchen and getting them to gobble them all up. That way the protein isn't wasted and I don't have to touch the yucky things.

The plan seems agreeable to Yoko, Marigold and Hillary who swing into action and start enthusiastically pecking at the little white maggots.

Only then do I look up and see Pearl's friend Willa, who has stayed the night, standing behind me looking on in horror. I'm not sure, but I have a fair idea that Willa has never seen hens in a kitchen eating maggots.

'Oh hi, Willa you're up early,' I said, doing my best to stand in front of the offending hens.

'Morning,' she replied, not sure whether to laugh out loud or keep it inside for risk of offending me.

I then realised that she may very well go home and tell her parents the hilarious story of Wendyl, the hens and the maggots.

'Look,' I said in a soft voice I hope encourages a sense of secrecy. 'Best you don't tell Mum and Dad about this eh?' I finished. 'Doesn't happen often.'

Willa smiled and gurgled her gorgeous laugh before running off to tell Pearl.

I didn't exactly get an agreement from her, but I know her parents fairly well and I'm sure they wouldn't have passed judgement even if they had heard about the maggot incident.

Once the maggots are all cleaned up and I have doused the floor in vinegar I remember that I haven't saved any tomato seed for next year. This is a slightly complicated process because you have to scoop out the tomato pulp with the seeds in it, put it in a jar with some water and wait for mould to grow.

At this stage someone in my house usually throws it out because it stinks and they naturally think it's rotten. But the mould is rotting away the protective coating of the tomato seeds which can prevent them from sprouting. So you let it rot, then rinse it all off, and you should have some not too shabby seeds that you then dry out for a few days on some paper towels. Which is when someone else in my family throws them out, not noticing the tiny seeds on what they think is a dirty kitchen towel. Sometimes it takes me about three goes before I get my precious seed. But it's worth it, because you know that in October, when you plant them into their little seed-raising pots, they will grow tomatoes that will grow good and strong in my soil with my garden's unique conditions. This is just one of the marvels of nature and on the few occasions when I have supplemented my tomato plants with some from the garden centre, it's the new ones that suffer from diseases like blight.

Other seeds in your garden are easier to save but it does mean you have a fairly ugly looking plant for a few months while it gets to the seed deposit stage. I often leave parsley, rocket, coriander and silverbeet to go to seed because I will use these over and over again in my garden so it is worth having the strange looking plants hanging about for a while.

To gather those seeds you simply wait until the pod is dry and wizened, then clip them at the bottom of the stem, put their heads in a paper bag and shake the hell out of them. You should end up with a fine collection of seed in the bottom of the bag.

By the end of March, the hens have thoroughly dug over my gardens and the plots are ready for me to dig deep, turn the soil, throw on some of my sweet compost made during the hot summer months, a bit of lime and blood and bone and let it sit for a few weeks before I plant for winter.

March also signals the arrival of fleas and, when Pearl was younger, nits. The heat of the summer means these little pests multiply furiously, and I am challenged to come up with more and more natural ways of dealing with them as the only other alternative is chemicals in our homes, on our children and on our pets.

It occurred to me that I have so successfully stopped bringing chemicals into my home, by making my own natural products, that the only chemical which still makes it through my front door is flea treatment for the pets, because you can't be having fleas. That's just unsanitary even by my standards.

Yet paying $69 a month to de-flea four animals and bringing into my house a slow acting poison which is highly toxic to bees, fish and birds (fipronil) and a growth retarding hormone (methoprene) into my home then happily squirting it onto our beloved pets and exposing the whole household to it, just doesn't make sense to me anymore.

For the animals I have found several natural methods that do work against fleas, but the secret is to keep up using them. If you're not using the power of chemicals then you have to be vigilant. Just as I say with my natural cleaners, if you're not using chemicals which magically make everything clean the minute you spray them on, you do have to combine natural cleaners with some elbow grease. With fleas you have to re-apply and combine all natural remedies and reapply them to see any results.

Instead of dripping chemicals on the cats I get busy with a flea comb. Cats love being combed every day and if you get into the habit then you are physically removing the fleas and their eggs.

For Shirl, I spray her with neat cider vinegar and leave it on for 20 minutes. Then I rinse it off. I do this every three days, three times and then do a maintenance dose every two weeks.

For Shirl and the three cats, Lucy, Sassy and Kitty, I also fight fleas from the inside. It is well known that fleas hate blood tainted with the taste of garlic and yeast. These two products also happen to be very good for animals, so I make up some flea biscuits for Shirl and flea powder which goes in with the cats' biscuits.

'I'm not sure the flea biscuits were a huge hit this afternoon,' my husband suggested as I was enthusiastically packing them into a cake tin.

'People who come around for a business meeting don't normally expect their employee to grab pongy yeast and garlic smelling dog biscuits out of the oven and shove them under their noses,' he continued the lecture.

'I was testing them out,' I offered weakly.

Visitors are never immune from becoming victims of my home economics experimentation. Along with my family they have tasted, slathered on, dipped into and bathed in my various concoctions with various degrees of consent. Occasionally the experiments have been carried out in what could only be described as an atmosphere of severe resentment prompting comparisons to the cruel and unwarranted testing on innocent animals carried out by cosmetic companies. Just for the record, to date, no one has been blinded in the making of my products. Someone did once get a rash, but we won't talk about that.

You also have to be aware that fleas actually spend more time off your animal than on them and they make their homes in pet bedding or in the cracks of your floors. So for that I sprinkle food-grade diatomaceous earth, a naturally occurring, chalk-like rock, which I also use on the hens.

It is safe to everyone except insects, which get coated in the powder. It cuts their waxy coating and they dehydrate within 48 hours. You can also sprinkle it on your pets.

When all these remedies are used together you will keep fleas at bay, but — and this happens to me every year — if you stop combing, sprinkling, spraying and baking biscuits for a week or two, you can expect the fleas to make a comeback, especially in March, when it is hot and humid and the breeding conditions are perfect. That is when I disappear to the caravan and Paul secretly flea bombs the house without telling me. So much for chemical-free living, but each year I try, fail and am determined to try harder next summer.

We have another consideration, which is that Pearl and Paul both have an allergy to flea and mosquito bites and for Pearl this means that her skin has difficulty healing. By March she is covered in itchy, sore bites — the culmination of a summer's attacks. She has to go on antibiotics, the only time in the year she needs them, as she never comes down with any common colds, flu or stomach bugs. Each time I get more and more frustrated that this has to happen. One year we are all hoping we will get through without the flea bombs, without the antibiotics and without the fleas!

When Pearl and the rest of the kids were younger they

would come home from school in March with nits. Every parent has to deal with this at some stage in their child's schooling and on the first day of school, you can almost mark on your calendar that four weeks later those nits will reappear after you've had a great six week holiday without them.

Nits are like fleas, you can treat them naturally but you have to keep at it. I can remember lining up all four of our older children in the kitchen and combing them all every other night. At the time I was editing a women's magazine and doing long hours. I had better things I could have been doing as soon as I got home from work, but the first rule of nits is to get out the comb and use it every other night for two weeks. You must also wash the bed linen every few days in hot water and add a dash of tea tree oil in the final rinse water.

One night while I was combing Pearl's hair I was drowning the nits in a glass of water next to me as I was finding them. We were both watching television and I was obviously engrossed in the programme because I took a long drink out of the glass next to me.

'Mum,' said Daniel in shock, 'I think you just drank the nit water.'

I was out of the lounge so fast and reaching for some fresh water to drink and then had to sit there for the next hour trying not to think about all the nits fighting for their lives in my stomach.

There are many natural nit shampoos and treatments available now and I urge you to use them in combination with the combing, but you can make your own. I buy a cheap, preferably unscented shampoo and conditioner and add tea-tree oil to it. I also drip tea-tree oil on our children's brushes, so that when they brush their hair a light coating will penetrate it and deter the nits.

Flies drive me absolutely nuts, and unfortunately with hens, come flies. As I sit writing this at the caravan, the flies are especially bad in the heat of March and I must confess that after putting out bowls of lavender oil and slathering myself in it, they are still coming back for more and I am, shamefully, spraying the little buggers with fly spray. I know how not Nana that is. I used to have a really cool plastic fly curtain like the ones they have in takeaway shops but I can't find it, so until I can replace it we live with the flies.

I do know that certain essential oils repel flies – citronella is one, as are lavender and eucalyptus. But you have to put a lot of it out and get it into the air somehow. Oil burners are one way, spraying it around is another or you could leave it in lots of little bowls around the house. You can wipe it on surfaces, or light incense. In my experience it takes a hell of a lot of essential oils to make a fly think twice. I know this because one hot summer's afternoon the kitchen was full of flies and Paul and I were making a huge batch of my lavender laundry liquid. When we do this the whole house takes on the odour of lavender oil and it's actually very soothing.

'Look, no flies,' I said to Paul after about 10 minutes.

They had all disappeared. But we had also gone through about 100 ml of lavender oil while making our laundry liquid.

I've had marginal success with soaking ribbons in lavender or citronella oil and then hanging them up from lampshades and in open doorways, but they last for about half an hour and then the flies come back.

I do have a recipe for an outdoor fly trap (see page 138) that seems to keep them away, and there's good old fly-paper like Nana used to make. When I tried it the flies got caught alright but I found myself just a little bit too much of a modern miss to enjoy seeing bits of sticky paper stuck with dead flies hanging in my kitchen.

My mother tells me that when she was a child they had a gecko that lived in their kitchen on a string suspended across the ceiling. His job was to catch flies and that's what he did. A great old-fashioned idea for those of you who are game but my house is mad enough with chickens, cats and dogs running about, I just don't need a pet lizard — especially one that might climb down and into my bed. This happened when I was a child and my brother Mark kept geckos in his bedroom. One escaped and decided my bed was the nicest place to rest for a while just as I hopped into bed for the night. I've had trouble with lizards, snakes and anything vaguely reptilian ever since.

Nana also would have used a fly swat. I can remember as a child watching adults who were rather adept with the old swat and then feeling vaguely ill as they hung it back up on the wall, still smeared with the remains of dead flies.

I've also bought one of those electric tennis racket fly swats that zaps the fly when you hit it, but who has the time to run around swatting flies? I had hoped the kids might like it, but after one day of fly killing it was discarded into the cupboard.

In recent years, pyrethrum sprays have come on the market and these do work. They are aerosol cans which you set and they spurt out a spray of supposedly natural fly deterrent every few minutes. I used one for a while until I realised pyrethrum is natural but it is a toxin. It's toxic to flies but also bees, fish, pets and us. Then I looked at the chemicals they add to the pyrethrum to get it to spray and suspend in the air. I came home from that research trip, walked into the house, picked up the can and threw it in the bin much to Paul's annoyance.

'It's the first day of autumn today,' announced Pearl in the kitchen one morning.

136

'Finally an end to the heat, the flies, the humidity,'
she commented. Pearl has a thing about the weather and the
seasons. She reads the weather page in the newspaper every day
and always notices seasonal changes as they happen.

'I don't know if I'm ready for it to be cold again,' I said,
remembering last winter.

'Just think, Mum, cosy fires, yummy stews, and you
making bread again.'

She had a point. We have a big wood burner which heats
the whole house, and for some reason in winter I make bread,
probably for the comforting warm smell of the yeast.

But before the cold sets in we have a few birthdays to take
care of next month. April is always about babies.

Fly Paper

¼ cup golden syrup

½ cup sugar

Mix the ingredients in a bowl and then paint or spread
on long strips of brown paper. Leave to dry on a tray
and then hang where flies are a problem.

Outdoor Fly Trap

Mix some blood and bone with water and put in the
bottom of plastic bag. Seal the top and then poke a few
holes in it just large enough for a fly to get in. Hang
from a tree and wait for the blood and bone to go off.
Make sure it is hanging a long way from the house!

Arrabiata

2 teaspoons olive oil

2 garlic cloves, peeled and finely chopped

5 tomatoes, chopped

½ lemon, zest only

½ teaspoon crushed dried chilli flakes, or two fresh chillies

2 teaspoons balsamic vinegar

1 teaspoon caster sugar

To make the sauce, heat oil in a medium saucepan. Stir in garlic and chopped tomatoes until warmed through. Add lemon zest, chilli, vinegar and sugar. Simmer for 10 minutes and pour into the sterilised jars right to the top while hot. Shake them slightly and push a skewer down to release any air bubbles that have formed.

When you have sealed the jars with preserving rings and lids and the sauce has cooled, the lids should be concave, proving that they have been well sealed. If not, you'll need to try again.

Quick Tomato Pasta Sauce (to eat freshly cooked, not preserved!)

1 kg tomatoes

4 cloves garlic

4 tablespoons cream

handful of basil

salt and pepper, to taste

grated parmesan, to sprinkle

Throw the tomatoes into a roasting dish along with the garlic cloves, which have been peeled and sliced. Spray some olive oil over them and put under the grill until you are sure they look burned to a crisp. You want the skin to be really black so that the sugars in the tomatoes caramelise and sweeten up. Put the unpeeled tomatoes and garlic in a bowl and mash with a fork. Tear up the basil leaves and throw them in and then stir in the

cream and salt and pepper. Pour onto freshly cooked
pasta and throw some parmesan on the top.

Paul's Oregano Cheese on Toast

Toast thick bread slices in the toaster. Spread one side
with butter, top with grated tasty cheese, sprinkle each
slice with at least a teaspoon of dried and crumbled
oregano, and freshly ground black pepper. Grill until
top is crunchy.

Tea-tree Oil
Shampoo and Conditioner

Make your own tea-tree shampoo
and conditioner by buying any cheap brand from the
supermarket and dropping tea-tree oil into the bottles.
I use about 10 drops per small bottle but you can adjust
it so that it gives a good strong smell. Your children
need to use it from now on. It won't kill an infestation
of nits but it will help prevent another one occurring.

Preserving Tips

Preserving food is such a lovely old-fashioned way to make sure we get the best out of produce while it is in season. Before the days of freezers, our nanas would bottle and preserve all their garden produce while it was in season and bursting with goodness. Then for months on end their families would be nourished and nurtured by it. These days it's a wonderful alternative to freezing fruit and vegetables because I think the flavours are nicer. If you don't have a garden you can buy produce at good prices in season and save a lot of money for just a little input of time. Here are some hints and tips for getting the best out of preserving.

- The principle of preserving is to heat the food up to a high heat which then destroys any bacteria that might be present. You then need to get it into a sterilised jar which then seals in a vacuum, meaning no bacteria can grow.
- This means everything has to be clean, clean, clean so wash your hands often, make sure your boards and utensils are washed and ready.
- Don't include any rotten parts of the fruit or vegetable — cut them out to avoid the bacteria getting in the mix.
- Adding lemon is a great idea as it makes the mix slightly acidic and therefore less likely to harbour germs.
- It is best to sterilise your jars at the same time as you are cooking up your recipe so that they are both hot at the same time.
- To sterilise your jars, wash in hot soapy water and rinse clean with hot water. Place the jars in an oven heated to 110°C and leave for five minutes. You can also place

the metal rings but leave the seals out as the plastic will melt. Wash them thoroughly and pop them in some boiling water for a few minutes.

- For sauces and jams the easiest method to use is the hot method where you cook the food, pour it into hot sterilised jars, place the lids on and seal. As the food cools a vacuum will be created causing the metal seal to pull inwards to form a concave shape. This is how you know your preserving has been successful.

- Another more old-fashioned method is called the overflow method. You place the food in sterilised jars and fill to the top so that it slightly overflows the jar. You then wipe the rim clean and seal the jar.

- If you are just wanting to pack fruit into a jar without cooking first then you can do this using the water bath method. Simply pack the sterilised jars with the raw fruit such as tomatoes or plums and cover each layer with a sugar-syrup solution, wine or juice. Seal the jar with vacuum seals, loosely screw on the metal bands and then place in a large saucepan or roasting dish filled with water so that it comes three-quarters of the way up the jars. Bring the water to the boil and cook for about 30 minutes. Once the syrup is bubbling and the fruit looks cooked remove from the bath and screw the lids on as tightly as you can. When they cool a vacuum should form.

- You can also seal with paraffin wax but you have to make extra sure there are no gaps left for air to enter and that the wax comes right to the top of the jar so that it is easy to get the wax off when you need to.

- When you have poured your food into the jars get a skewer and run it down inside the jars to release any air bubbles which might be in the jars, or alternatively thump the jar on the bench a few times.

- You can find second-hand jars and preserving equipment like pans in second-hand stores and op shops, but do buy the rings and lids new as they are most likely a bit rusty and could contaminate the food.
- If you are making a pickle or chutney, some people like to pour vinegar over the jars before filling to prevent fermentation.
- Be aware that you are preserving, not mummifying! Your jars will have a shelf life. Most jams and pickles will last for a year, chutneys and relishes for about 18 months. So make sure you date all your preserves and if you are at all unsure about a jar discard the contents rather than take the risk.
- Try to use stainless steel cookware as other metals can affect the flavour.
- Most recipes call for sugar in vast amounts and there's a reason for this — it is a preservative. Don't be tempted to replace it with another substance to save on calories.
- Keep all preserves in a cool, dark place. It's tempting to have them all on display but you will only shorten their shelf life if you do.
- Make sure you are in a good mood. If you are rushing or don't really feel like cooking your preserves you will miss out on the joy of a few hours spent in the kitchen.

Dog Oil

Make up this oil and rub it into your dog, and on their collar.

50 ml olive oil

3 drops lemon essential oil

3 drops orange essential oil

3 drops citronella essential oil

Mix all the ingredients together. Use it every two days and your dog will love the massage, it will soothe itchiness and deter fleas. This should be enough for two applications for a large dog, more for smaller breeds. Do not use on cats as they hate orange oil.

Doggy Flea Treats

3 teaspoons Maggi beef stock powder

3 ½ cups wholemeal flour

½ cup wheatgerm

½ cup bran

½ cup linseed

⅔ cup brewer's yeast

2 tablespoons garlic granules (in spice aisle of your local supermarket)

2 eggs

1 ½ cups hot water

Mix all the ingredients together except the eggs and water. Mix in the eggs then slowly add the hot water stirring all the time until you have a workable dough – the stickier the better. Roll out, cut into shapes and place on a greased tray. Bake at 180°C for 20 minutes, then turn off the oven, prop the door open a little with a wooden spoon and leave to harden overnight or at least a few hours.

For large dogs – like my Shirl – give 2 to 3 biscuits a day, smaller dogs 1 or 2 biscuits each day is fine.

De-flea Powder

100 grams brewer's yeast

30 grams garlic powder (not garlic salt!)

1 tablespoon bran

1 tablespoon wheatgerm

Whizz together in a food processor and store in an air tight container. Feed I teaspoon per day per cat. I just throw about half a cup in with a box of biscuits and give it a good shake up. The powder attaches itself to the sticky biscuits and the cats don't seem to mind a bit.

APRIL

April is always about babies for me.

On 30 April, our first granddaughter Lila was born and we were two very happy grandparents. When Paul's son Joel and his partner Gemma sat down at our big kauri kitchen table and told Pearl that she needed to leave the room because the grown-ups were going to have a chat, I immediately knew what was coming.

'You guys are going to be grandparents,' said Joel quietly.

Paul and I leapt into the air and high-fived each other, then sat down, a little shocked at our reaction. But not as shocked as the two parents-to-be sitting across from us.

'We thought you might have some misgivings, we're so young,' said Joel.

'Not too young! Same as I was when I had you!' said Paul

enthusiastically. 'Good age to have babies, 25, bloody good age.'

It just seemed like such a lovely thing to happen to our family. And with Paul just 50 and me in my mid-forties we felt quite blessed to be grandparents at an age when we could still enjoy the grandchildren.

I went quite silly and immediately bought a job lot of baby clothes and equipment on TradeMe, sparking a rumour in the neighbourhood that I was having a late-life baby after I was seen carrying it all inside.

Paul immediately started making plans for which day of the week would be best to babysit, as he fully intended for us to be active caregivers from day one. Then he started compiling a suitable playlist on his iPod for just such occasions.

And then she arrived.

As we left the hospital I looked at my beaming husband and had a moment. So this is what it is all about, I thought as he paid for the parking. This is the payoff for those times when it was tough and rather than walk away we pulled up our sleeves and got on with the hard work of commitment, creating and holding a blended family together and launching all those children off into the world in the best state we could.

You turn up at Auckland Hospital on a bright sunny morning and hold in your arms the most beautiful smelling, reassuringly plump and healthy bundle of beauty. Just when your house starts to empty of children, the next generation arrives to fill the rooms with their small but significant energy.

A few months later, we would have another moment, Grandpa and I. Our dreams of spending most days cuddling and cooing over Lila, dancing her around the room and rolling around on the floor bathed in the joy of infanthood were not panning out.

'I don't think she likes me,' Paul said, holding his

148

screaming granddaughter as tightly as he could and rocking her in that special way which has settled all other children before her, earning him the nickname of 'Baby Whisperer'.

Our granddaughter had other ideas. She'd give us energy all right, but not in the way which had filled our fantasies. It would seem our big house with all its noise and madness is a bit overwhelming for our baby. She arrives at the door full of smiles, placid and gorgeous as usual but once she's over the threshold all hell breaks loose.

Then suddenly I found in the dark recesses of my brain a well thumbed volume of baby care tips gleaned from my four babies, one of whom was also fond of a bit of quiet and calm. I was very pleased to find it.

'You can come and look at her now,' I told my husband once Lila was settled and happy with the three things I had gently asked her parents to bring with her. Her familiar pram, her mum's T-shirt so she could smell her and her new friend the lion that sings *Merry Christmas*.

He returned from the other end of the house where he had exiled himself with the dog – who would shake and quiver the minute Lila cried – and peered into the pram.

'Moo-moo' whispered Lila.

By the time Lila was 10 months old, she had settled into a routine with us and her other adoring grandparents who are just as keen on spending time with her as we are. Before I knew it I found myself spending the weekend rolling around on the floor shouting 'ga ga', singing 'If you're happy and you know it,' while clapping my hands with a loony grin plastered on my face, and batting a giant blow-up soccer ball around the floor.

This would usually be evidence that I was either still drunk from Friday night, or involved in a past-life regression designed to purge myself of dark demons involving abuse with a blow up ball and bad singing.

It was neither. I was simply discovering the fact that in my mid-forties two days of floor time is just what an old girl needs when she has a 10-month-old granddaughter to stay.

In the great scheme of life it would seem that the energy expended and the brain stimulation required by a nearly one-year-old are exactly equal to those of a 46-year-old woman called Wendyl. Two days of reading picture books, throwing things around, eating mashed up food and grunting is now my idea of the perfect weekend.

Who knew that two naps a day at approximately 9 am and 1 pm could be so perfectly in tune with my need to lie down and close my eyes? That when you wake early, as most seniors do, so too does Lila, beaming at you from her cot in the dark at 6 am when you stop by to check her on the way to make a cup of tea. And how great is a lavender bath followed by bed at 7 pm?

This was all very new to me. When I had my own babies in my early twenties, I don't remember ever sitting on the floor with them. I was always too busy to stop, rushing out the door to work, racing in the door to housework and dinner and resenting having to stay home on a Saturday night while my mates partied hard before ringing the next day with tales of debauchery at 2 am — the precise time I was getting up to feed my baby.

I would look at my chubby, happy babies crawling around and think they were just lovely, but the last thing I would do was sit down on the floor and join them. Now, it seems, is my time for sitting.

'Are you still down there?' said Pearl, discovering Lila and I engrossed in the dust balls and discarded pens we had found under the couch.

'She might want some fresh air at some stage,' suggested Paul hopefully.

'Mum, you're doing a very good impression of a stranded whale,' said Hannah, adding that it was 4 pm and I was still in my pyjamas.

'Rush, rush, rush, that's all it is with you lot,' I responded, picking up Lila and suggesting that we might like to roll around on the deck for a change of scene. When did looking after a baby have to be an event?' I tossed over my shoulder as Lila and I collapsed in the shade.

By the time Joel and Gemma picked Lila up on the Sunday night I felt as if I had been at one of those exotic health farms. All those lovely naps, all that organic soft food, the singing and the holding hands. So restorative.

'She can come back anytime,' I cooed as I attempted to get up off the lounge floor for the first time that weekend and failed.

'Are you all right?' asked Joel, no doubt alarmed that I might have hit the bottle from the stress of looking after his child. Either that or run a marathon during her afternoon nap.

'It's okay,' said Paul. 'She's just been making up for lost time.'

Shortly after her weekend stay Lila started walking and we soon learned that running around after a moving baby in mid-life is quite a different story to being a young parent in your early twenties.

Our bodies, having had 20 years off changing nappies, playing hide-and-seek, pushing strollers and lifting a heavy toddler up and down several hundred times a day, quite naturally go into shock and shut down when required to do it again.

I was in just such a prone position one weekend when

Lila was picked up after a 24-hour stay. While she performed what can only be interpreted as a delightful haka on speed at the welcome sight of her returning parents, I found myself prone on the couch and unable to move.

'Everything all right?' Gemma inquired thoughtfully as I grudgingly moved my feet up the couch to make room for her and Joel to sit down.

'Wine?' I responded, instructing the adult nearest the kitchen to get glasses and a bottle. That happened to be Paul, who was still standing, despite having done the lion's share of lifting, bending and chasing our toddler.

I let him see them to the door.

'Another wine?' he suggested on his return.

Which is how we ended up a mere two hours later at a party down the road doing our own version of a haka on speed, only we were on the wine, which made for a slightly messier rendition. One of us may have fallen over at some point.

One of us may have also got involved in far too many conversations involving the word 'me' and the phrase 'did I tell you about my granddaughter?' As we stumbled back home through the neighbourhood in the early hours I wondered out loud how one person, namely myself, could morph so efficiently from adoring and attentive grandma to tragic middle-aged woman walking into a hedge in just a few hours.

I was relieved there were no children at home to witness our arrival as we stumbled up the steps with someone's herb garden in my hair.

We sat at the kitchen table and realised that what we had just witnessed was a rather extreme reaction to having a toddler in the house again. Over the 24-hour period we had revisited those endless hours, days and years when we were slaves to our babies. Never letting them out of our sight, feeding and entertaining, worrying and wondering, our antennae set to full power for maximum reaction and immediate attention. Then suddenly we were free again. Free to be those crazy old people who can pretty much do whatever we like, when we like, how we like.

'I miss her,' Paul mumbled as we went to bed, both pausing to look at her empty cot, her teddy lying discarded in one corner, a single sock left behind in the other.

'Me too,' I winced as I tried to get into bed without something aching, not sure if the strenuous baby care or the hedge was to blame.

'Need more babies. Must get the kids onto it,' was the last thing he said before snoring his way through what was left of the night.

Lila still exhausts us but she also makes us laugh our heads off and she always heads straight for those chickens when she arrives, putting on her special garden shoes, just like Grandma's and calling out for the dog: 'Shirl, where are you?'

I grow strawberries in a tub for her every year and she also loves fresh peas, just out of the shell. She likes the cocktail tomatoes her mum grows, but isn't so keen on mine, and there is always a meal in the house for Lila when sweet corn is in season. She loves wrapping her teeth around a fresh cob. More recently her favourite food at Grandma and Grandpa's house is an omelette made out of the hen's eggs. I don't think there is a healthier food we could feed her.

When Lila arrived I started focusing my natural cleaning on natural babies. I don't think we realise just how many chemicals we subject our babies to right from birth. We wipe their bottoms with chemical baby wipes, we wash their clothes and nappies in laundry detergent leaving chemicals in the cloth, we bring them home to houses with air fresheners and fly sprays, and we heat up plastic bottles in microwaves, causing them to leach chemicals.

I don't use a microwave, simply because I believe that the method of heating the food kills off many of its nutrients. British food writer Delia Smith agrees, saying in *The Times* in 1990: 'I think it takes the soul out of food.'

I'm not sure I want my food to be heated in plastic containers whose molecular structure changes so that some of that substance may enter my food.

Lila was breastfed but when we needed to heat a bottle of breast milk, or later when she was on formula, we would simply put it in a pot of water on the stove, just like Nana did. It didn't take much longer. And actually Nana used to use glass bottles which, in my opinion, are much safer and they last longer.

After looking at the ingredients list for a popular baby-wash sold in the supermarket, I made up a baby-wash to put in Lila's bath. Joel and Gemma came back for repeat supplies over and over, until Lila got older and really needed some bubbles at bath time. That has proved to be a bit trickier so I'm still working on a natural bubble bath for babies.

Another thing I love making is my natural baby wipes. I always have a Tupperware container full of them for when Lila comes around but they are also really handy for cleaning up any messes, like the occasional chicken poo, left behind after they get inside the house. I also keep some in a resealable bag that I keep in my handbag. Paul calls them a 'bidet in a box' and thinks we should market them as a personal hygiene product. He has lots of good ideas, my husband, but I don't think this is one of them.

Then it was on to rashes. All babies get rashes of some sort, usually as a reaction to a new food or substance that they are being exposed to. For any rash I always try aloe vera gel first because it is marvellously soothing and effective. Putting oatmeal in baby's bath also helps and the chemist will sell you zinc oxide cream mixed with castor oil, which also works well. Of course, I recommend changing to my chemical-free baby-wipes!

You would think that being the nana I am, I would have wanted Lila to have cloth nappies and not the disposables which clog up our rubbish dumps. But on this subject I'm a realist, just as I am about breast-feeding versus bottle feeding. I tried cloth nappies with my children and just couldn't keep up. I tried breast-feeding with my first two children and just couldn't keep up. Some parents find that they can cope, but it does add an extra load on new parents, who are often already flat-out working and caring for children. It's a personal choice and if you've made the decision to use cloth nappies, I have some helpful tips for you at the end of the chapter. But the truth is I'd rather see parents having fun and spending time with their babies than slaving over a bucket of cloth nappies.

Our hen baby Matilda is leading a strange life in April. She is half grown and has to be separated from Hillary, Marigold and Yoko because the moment they see her they attack her. It seems chickens, unlike most other animals, have no maternal urges or the ability to accept strays and orphans.

I fashioned a sleeping box out of an old wooden cat cage we used to transport one of our cats back to Auckland from Sydney. Then I gave Matilda free rein of part of the garden, safely fenced off from the others. This seems to work well, so then I have supervised visits, where the other hens are allowed to come in and hang out with Matilda. I reason that if there are any dramas she will make such a noise that I can come running from my office to save her.

They spent a couple of days like this, happily digging and

scratching with Matilda, who was only occasionally chased away if she got too close to the older hens' food source.

'I think she's ready to join them,' I announced to the family one morning after a week of happy visitations. 'It's about time she became a proper hen.'

I plonked Matilda over the fence and made sure there were two sources of food and water as I have read that older hens will deprive the younger ones if forced to share.

All seemed to be going well with Matilda at one end and the hens at the other so I retired to the front deck with Paul for a coffee in the autumn sunshine.

Ten minutes later Pearl appeared pale-faced.

'Something's happening and it doesn't look good,' she said in a low voice.

I ran down the hall and out in the garden to find poor little Matilda cornered against a fence at the back of the garden with three huge hens running at her and pecking her. It reminded me of those terrible cock fights you see on old movies. Feathers and dust were flying everywhere. I rushed in and grabbed all three rather ungraciously by the feet and threw them into their coop where I locked them up. I've never been so rough with them, I usually pick them up gently, cooing and stroking, but I was in no mood for pleasantries. I followed the trail of black and white feathers until I found a clump of them, obviously pecked out in one go, and a petrified Matilda who was no longer my cute, tame pullet-in-training. She was very hard to catch and would only come near me after much coaxing with raisins.

Only then did I notice that no one else in the family had come out to help. Paul and Pearl had shot off, far away from the drama.

'Everything okay?' asked Paul peeking around the corner of the deck.

'Bloody hens, I hate them,' I ranted. 'What kind of animal doesn't look after their young? Madness.'

The awful thing was that Matilda hadn't made a sound. The only reason Pearl had been alerted was that Kitty, our matriarch cat, had run in and meowed at her persistently until she looked out into the garden, wondering if Kitty had caught a bird or a rat. Instead she had seen the beginnings of certain death.

When the dust had settled, I noticed that Kitty never left Matilda's side. The two of them would spend all day together on their side of the garden and seem to have formed some kind of cross-species alliance. Kitty has taken a close interest in Matilda ever since she arrived but I always thought that the hunter in her was simply casing out her next prey. But three months later I had to admit that she could have killed her from the first day we let Matilda out into the garden, and perhaps in her old age she had just taken a liking to the black and white hen.

'I wouldn't be surprised if we come out here one afternoon and find those two cuddling up in the sun,' I said to Pearl.

'Matilda even lies down in the sun like a cat,' she said pointing towards the lemon tree where Kitty and Matilda were having a nap.

And there was Matilda lying on her side with her feet stuck out just like a cat — something I've never seen the other hens do.

For the moment our baby hen/cat lives a rather feline existence where she shares food, grooms and dozes with the cats all day while the other hens, who I still haven't forgiven gaze through the fence, no doubt planning their next attack.

Paul's birthday arrives in the middle of the month on the 17th. I decided to make him something special for his bathroom cabinet. Ever since he was editor of *FQ Men*, which was a very stylish glossy fashion magazine for men, the bathroom cabinet has been full of male grooming products from eye gel, to firming moisture balm, hair gel, brightening serum, and pre-shave, during-shave and after-shave gel, balm and soother. Not to mention several heavily priced bottles of cologne. At first I was amused as Paul slowly turned from being the scruffy guy I first met into a metrosexual with more beauty products than his wife. But rather disturbingly, while I had long ago got the message about chemicals in beauty products, he was in his first flush of high-powered beauty marketing and bought it all, hook, line and sinker. He would come home from the office every day with a sample delivered to him by a cosmetic company and eagerly try it out and then he became addicted to one substance which claimed to 'help' his crow's feet. Despite my protestations he continued to spend a small fortune on it until he discovered the greatest remedy for wrinkly skin. Giving up his 35-year pack-a-day smoking habit. Almost overnight his skin plumped out and his wrinkles disappeared.

This birthday I was going to see if I could bring him a little closer to nature with a gift pack of natural solutions for the metrosexual. I made a very good hair gel, after-shave lotion, mouthwash and foot deodoriser and he pronounced them all a great success. And last time I looked in the bathroom cupboard, it was almost bare, apart from a few old samples he was hanging onto and a deodorant. I have yet to invent a deodorant that works.

One product we both discovered after Paul gave up smoking is an oil that heals just about everything on the skin. When Paul stopped smoking he developed an itchy skin condition which treatment from the doctor wasn't really helping. Obviously there were some pretty nasty toxins trying to get out of his body so he learned to live with it, knowing that one day it would clear up.

Then he was at the acupuncturist for a sore neck and she spotted the rash and dabbed some tamanu oil on. It went away within days. We now use it for everything from wound healing to rashes and even fungal complaints. It is my go-to oil when skin flares up. Tamanu oil comes from the nuts of the tamanu tree which grows throughout the South Pacific. Polynesian people have used it for centuries for everything from insect bites, sunburn, as a deodorant and for nappy rash. It has a strong, sweet nutty smell and is quite pleasant to use.

Another baby was born in April. On 7 April, 1992, Virginia – my daughter with my first husband Anthony Ellison – was born. She died three months later of cot death. I still pause on her birthday and take some time to think about her and what might have been. I imagine her now at 17 striding through life as beautiful as her siblings Daniel and Hannah, and probably giving me some grief as teenage girls do. I know that over at my parents' house, my mother always places a flower beneath the pohutukawa tree that has her ashes buried beneath it. On her 14th birthday Daniel and I went off and had tattoos done. Mine is on my left bicep and simply says 'Virginia 1992.' There will never be an April – or a month, or a week if I'm honest – when I don't think about her.

But with the arrival of Lila, April has taken on a new meaning and a new life, which I'm enjoying immensely. I get through the 7th, celebrate Paul's birthday on the 17th and then look forward to Lila's birthday on the 30th.

Aloe Vera Gel

If you have a plant at home —
everyone should have one to treat the occasional kitchen
burn — take a leaf and slice it down the middle. Open out
the leaves and scrape out the gel. Be careful not to get any
of the green liquid in the gel that comes out at the leaf
surface as this can be an irritant. Simply rub the gel on
and let it heal. Alternatively most health shops now stock
Aloe Vera gel, which will do the same job.

Zinc Oxide Cream

Most chemists sell simple jars of zinc oxide cream. The
cream will usually have some castor oil, paraffin or
lanolin mixed in with it.

Hair Gel

1 ½ teaspoons gelatine

250 ml warm water

10 drops essential oil — use your favourite ones.

This uses gelatine which is actually collagen and full of
protein so it can double as a hair strengthener as well.

Mix gelatine with water until it dissolves. Add 10
drops of your favourite essential oil such as lavender or
I use sandalwood for a blokey smell. Put aside for a few
hours to set and then tip into a blender and blend until
smooth.

If you like your gel a little less firm just use a teaspoon of gelatine. You can also dilute the gel with water in a sprayer for a natural holding hairspray.

Mouthwash

I don't trust the commercial mouthwashes as they contain ethanol and there has been some concern raised about it causing oral cancer. Also in recent years there have been recalls for some products because of safety concerns. This mouthwash does contain alcohol but only a little bit and you need it to spread the essential oil evenly through the mix and it also stimulates your gums. You'll have fresh breath for hours using this mix.

30 ml warm water

1 teaspoon lemon juice

1 teaspoon brandy

1 drop peppermint essential oil

Mix together and then swish around your mouth. If you have toothache or infection replace the peppermint oil with clove oil – only use one drop though, this oil is very powerful . . . oh and it tastes terrible!

Aftershave Splash

I'm reliably informed that most men these days just dab on a bit of cologne after shaving, but splashing on this mix gives the combined healing and antiseptic powers of witchhazel and rosewater as well as returning the skin to a neutral pH after using alkaline soap.

40 ml rosewater

40 ml witchhazel

10 ml vodka

8 drops bergamot essential oil

4 drops rosemary essential oil

1 teaspoon glycerine (add this for older men or those with dry skin as it
  adds extra moisturising, for oily skin, leave it out)

Mix all together, put in a nice bottle and splash away.

Foot Odour

Smelly feet and shoes are a problem for many men, yet they are really easy to fix with my favourite ingredient, baking soda, and this three step plan:

1. Get every pair of shoes and sprinkle inside liberally with some baking soda. Follow up with a few drops of tea-tree oil and leave overnight. In the morning shake out the powder. Do this treatment once a week to ensure you are killing off any fungus living in

the shoes. Also try to go barefoot as often as possible to give your feet a good airing.

2. Soak the feet as often as possible, even once a week, in a bucket of warm water with 2 tablespoons of sea salt and 2 tablespoons of baking soda added to it.

3. Mix 50 ml of base oil such as olive, almond or jojoba. Add to that 10 drops lavender essential oil and 10 drops tea-tree essential oil. Rub this oil into the feet, preferably in the morning before you put your socks on, as a deterrent to fungi and odours.

Hand Cleaner

Paul doesn't spend a lot of time under cars getting covered in grease so I didn't make this for him. But a man or a woman who spends time tinkering outside inevitably comes inside with dirty, greasy hands, and when they use commercial cleaners those hands get very dry indeed. I suggest they try first coating their hands in olive oil to release the grease and grime and then wash with ordinary soap.

Baby Bath Wash

Lila's mum and dad say this is their
favourite of all my inventions and Lila
just loves it in her bath. It's easy to make
and you know what is going on to your baby's skin.

400 ml water

80 ml rosewater

4 tablespoons grated 100% natural vegetable oil soap — look in your

health shop for a good bar

20 ml glycerine

10 drops lavender essential oil

Bring the water to the boil in a small saucepan and then
add the grated soap. Stir until all the soap is melted
then take off the heat and allow to cool a little until just
warm. Add the rest of the ingredients and pour into a
squeeze bottle. Depending on the soap you use this may
cool into a gel or remain quite liquid. Simply squeeze
some into the bath while you're running it. This wash
will not bubble but cleans and moisturises baby's skin
beautifully.

Baby Wipes

I first made these with kitchen towels but after testing them on Lila they weren't quite tough enough. I also thought a recyclable option would be good too. One of my newsletter readers kindly suggested I use rolls of Chux cloths which you can buy for $15 at some bulk bin stores. You can then wash the cloths and re-use them. Here are two options to try. The witchhazel is a fantastic antiseptic which has a great effect on itchy or inflamed skin and the rosewater not only smells great but is also anti-bacterial and antiseptic. In Morocco they pour it on their hands to wash them. It also balances out the pH levels on the skin.

½ cup water

1 tablespoon rosewater

1 tablespoon witchhazel

1 teaspoon aloe vera gel (optional)

Mix the ingredients together. Pour a little of the mixture into the bottom of a plastic container with an airtight lid. Rip up a few small kitchen towels or Chux cloths and place them in the bottom of the container and pour a little more of the liquid every time you have about 10 towels laid down. Continue layering until you have soaked all the cloths then put on the lid.

For travel packs you can simply pop a few into a resealable plastic bag and pour some of the mixture in with them.

Baby Clothes Pre-wash

Most clothes we buy in the shops have been treated with some sort of preservatives or additives to keep them looking good on the rack. Before your baby gets anywhere near new clothing you need to soak the clothing and then wash it and preferably hang it on the line to dry in the sun. This pre-soak is a great for all new baby clothes followed by a natural fabric softener in the final rinse to remove any hint of chemicals.

Soak the clothes in the washing machine bowl to which you have added ½ cup of washing soda. In the morning wash as usual and then to the final rinse add the following fabric softener mixture:

1 cup baking soda

1 cup white vinegar

2 cups water

Nappy Washing

Most parents who use cloth nappies say that once you get into a routine it's no more difficult than using disposables, and of course, you get to feel like a saint for not filling our landfills with plastic. The mistake many cloth-nappy users make is that they think they have to use commercial soakers and bleaches to keep them clean. What you are actually doing is loading up the cloth with chemicals which don't wash out and can cause nappy rash. Here is my tried and true recipe for washing nappies.

1. Soak soiled nappies in a bucket to which you have added ½ cup of baking soda.

2. When you wash them in the machine use my laundry liquid or another natural product but use half as much as you would for a normal wash.

3. In the final rinse add 1 cup white vinegar to rinse out all the soap residue.

4. Hang in the sun to dry. Sunlight is a powerful, free and completely natural bleaching agent. If you have some tough stains to remove try dabbing with lemon juice and salt and placing them outside in direct sunlight. You'll be amazed at the results.

Nappy Rash Cream

All babies get nappy rash at some stage and it is tempting to rush off to the chemist or doctor to get a commercial cream. But there are two very simple, natural alternatives – aloe vera gel and zinc oxide cream. Make sure when you are cleaning baby that you add some oatmeal to the bathwater to help heal the skin and use warm olive oil to wipe the bottom during nappy changes.

won't eat anything with more than five ingredients on the label. I won't eat anything my nana wouldn't recognise. These are the two statements I decided I would live by during the month of May. These are not original ideas and they are both open to some very logical disputes. For a long time now, because of my rejection of chemicals in my house through the use of commercial cleaners I have come to regard food with the same suspicious eye. Just because it has a label listing its ingredients or the words 'natural' or 'healthy' doesn't mean it is good for me. I read both *The Omnivore's Dilemma* and *In Defense of Food*, written by American journalist Michael Pollan, and his discoveries about the over-processing of food made sense.

When it comes to advice, I am always very ready to take it from a journalist like Pollan rather than a nutritionist, scientist, government agency or doctor. Primarily I am biased towards journalists because I am one, but also because the good ones look into a topic from an objective position and reveal all the information for you to consider, from both sides of the argument.

In Pollan's case he goes in, gets the information and then summarises it. Good journalists also write in a style the average person can understand, unlike scientists and government agencies. Pollan is not the only person out there saying that when health experts and government agencies tell us what to eat, they are not always right. Governments are targeted by large industry lobby groups and major food producers, such as farmers and growers. Imagine what would happen if tomorrow our government put out a recommendation that as a nation we should vastly reduce our red meat protein intake to half of what we eat? This is what is advised by most nutritionists — eat less red meat, more fish, more plants. But we are a nation of farmers — someone has to eat all that meat they are producing when exports aren't going so well.

I'm also not sure when it became okay to feed our children ingredients we don't understand because they are listed in code. Three numbers tell us nothing about an additive until we sit down at a computer and look it up or carry around a long list with us when we shop so that we can interpret the codes on the go.

Food additives are usually added to food to make it last longer on the shelf, taste differently, look more appealing or to keep it crisp, dry and crunchy. The main food in the package may be a natural product, such as potato in potato chips, but surrounding it can be dozens of chemicals simply to make it do things it wouldn't be able to do naturally.

In my opinion, we have a right to know what they are, without having to learn a new language of coded numbers, so

I am the one with my reading glasses on holding up the aisle in the supermarket as I exhaustively examine labels. Not many people know how to do this, so I am going to tell you.

The order in which the ingredients are listed tells you how much of each food is in the product you are about to buy. For some potato chips it will be potatoes, oil, salt, because most of the food you are about to eat is potato, followed by the oils they are cooked in followed by the salt they are seasoned with. I will eat those potato chips. They have three ingredients I understand and thankfully they are still available.

For ingredients you don't understand I urge you to get on your computer and do an analysis of the most common processed foods you and your children eat. Be careful with your research on the internet, though. There are thousands of websites claiming ingredients cause cancer, diabetes and allergies, which aren't substantiated and the sites are often pushing a particular cause or belief which means the information you are reading is not always true. There are also hundreds of websites claiming all additives are safe. I encourage you to seek good information and make your own mind up. I use Wikipedia which I regard as a well-monitored and reasonably non-biased information source but even then be aware of possible biases.

If you type in 'List of food additives, Codex Alimentarius' (Latin for 'food code' or 'food book') you will find a list of every code number assigned to food additives, and the name of the chemical it stands for. You can look up the code number e.g. 621 and find it stands for monosodium glutamate or MSG. You can then click on that name and it will take you to a full description of the substance.

Read through and look out for subject lines such as 'Sensitivities and Allergies' and 'Possible Health Effects'. This information is produced by the Codex Alimentarius

Commission, which was established by the World Health Organisation and is recognised by the World Trade Organisation as an international reference point for the resolution of disputes concerning food safety and consumer protection.

The irony is that you, as a consumer, have all the information at your fingertips in the form of an ingredients label with lots of codes on it. You then have to go home and look them up to find out what they represent. I doubt many people have the time to do this.

But I did one afternoon when I brought home a pack of Eta Uppercuts It's a Matter of Taste Kettles Succulent Roast Lamb & Mint Flavoured Potato Chips, with the rather ominous statement on the packaging *"They said we couldn't make them taste like the real thing"...You were saying?'* and on the back *'Those Uppercuts Kettles have the most sensational crunch and damn fine flavours I've ever tasted! So "tuck in"...'*

I have no idea who they are quoting with any of these statements and feel sure that they have simply made them up and put them in quote marks to make me feel like the package is talking to me.

I was about to find out how that roast lamb and mint — a dish about as Nana as they come and a traditional meal for decades on Kiwi tables — could be turned into a flavour.

I opened the bag and peered inside. A strong smell of something meaty came up to meet me and I turned the bag to face the wall as I read the ingredients:

Potatoes
That's good — the biggest ingredient in the bag is potatoes.
Vegetable oil [antioxidants (319, 330)]
I'm not sure what the oil is, which is a shame, but it does tell me that there are two preservatives in that oil to stop it

going rancid. Antioxidant 319 is tertiary-Butylhydroquinone (TBHQ) a synthetic preservative. In very high doses, it is thought to be acutely toxic to lab animals.

Antioxidant 330 is citric acid. It prevents bacteria growth and gives the citric/sour flavour. If produced naturally citric acid is fine. If artificially produced the production process can involve sulphuric acid, which could leave sulphites that some people are allergic to.

I reach into the bag to take out a chip for further investigation. It looks good and before I know it I have put it in my mouth where I crunch down on the thin chip and taste something salty, yeasty, and meaty, but not really lamb and mint. I try another one and there is the lamb and yes, a sort of slightly acidic aftertaste you could compare to mint sauce. That'll be the citric acid. I take another one. . . these chips are very moreish.

Flavour: [salt, milk solids, yeast extracts

I can live with that, all natural products I know. Another chip goes in and I really begin to get a stronger flavour of that lamb and mint. I'm not sure if it is just that I've convinced myself of the lamb/mint combo or whether I really do taste it. My mouth is full of meaty, salty, acid explosions as I crunch away happily.

Flavour enhancers (621,635,631,627)

Additive 621 is monosodium glutamate or MSG. This substance has had a troubled past and is used commonly in takeaway food. There is anecdotal evidence that it can cause asthma in some people and the New Zealand government requires it to be labelled.

Additive 635 is disodium 5'-ribonucleotides. According to Wikipedia, this has been linked with skin rashes (ranging from mild to severe) up to 30 hours after ingestion. It is recommended that no food containing disodium ribonucleotides should be consumed by gout or asthma sufferers. Neither of these statements on Wikipedia have citations so I take them with a grain of salt.

Additive 631 is disodium inosinate, which doesn't appear to have any health concerns listed. However I read with interest that both 631 and 635 are used in processed foods to give the taste of umami, which is a Japanese word for flavour or taste, and is commonly referred to as savouriness. It is a basic taste of broth or meaty flavour. So the meaty flavour I am experiencing as I munch on the succulent roast lamb and mint chips is probably just the flavour receptors on my tongue responding to the reaction caused by chemicals hitting my tongue.

I begin to feel a little ill, but I still reach for another crunchy chip from the bag.

Additive 627 is disodium guanylate which is naturally derived from fish. Great news. But it is recommended that it not be given to babies under the age of twelve weeks, and should also generally be avoided by asthmatics and people with gout. I munch away wondering why anyone would give a baby under three-months-old a chip, but I guess it happens.

Hydrolysed Vegetable Protein
This is basically boiled-down maize, soy or wheat.
Lactose
This is sugar derived from milk.
Sugar
This is most likely to have come from corn syrup.
Acidity Regulator 262
This is sodium acetate, which is a chemical often used in salt and vinegar chips to get the vinegar taste — in this case the vinegar in mint sauce. It is also used in heat pads.
Vegetable Oil {Antioxidant (306)}
This seems to be Vitamin E and in there as a preservative. I'm

not sure why vegetable oil is listed again under flavourings.
Herbs

Anticaking agent 551

This is silicon dioxide or silica, which is not a food. It passes through the digestive system and I can only presume it is in there to stop the ingredients clumping.

I pause for a moment and realise that during my investigation I have managed to munch my way through half a packet of chips and I'm not feeling so good. The initial buzz and crunch of flavour has given way to a dead weight in my stomach and I am reminded of how I have felt at parties when I've sat too close to the chip bowl and eaten more than I needed. Is this a feeling of too much rich food? Too many potatoes? Or too many chemicals? I don't know the answer, but I know I don't want to eat anymore. Those thin slivers of potatoes that were so delicious half an hour ago, now taste awful.

Perhaps it is just that I have found out too much about them. I continue researching, realising that I am now getting to the tiniest ingredients, the last on the list, the ones that make up the least of the contents, and finally we are finding a few things apart from potatoes that Nana might recognise:
Malt Extract

A sweetener usually derived from barley.

Maltodextrin

Sugar derived from corn starch.

Spice

Starch (wheat tapioca)

Flavour — no numbers or explanation provided so this could be pretty much anything.

Spice Extract — again no numbers or explanation provided. And that's where I get to put the closing] which started all the way up after that word Flavour.

I have just spent two hours eating and researching a packet of chips. Had I just bought the packet of chips with three ingredients: potatoes, oil, salt, I would have saved myself 25 additives and flavour enhancers put in the bag to make them taste like roast lamb and mint. As well as avoiding feeling uncomfortably full and not very well.

I am reminded of a chapter in *Fast Food Nation*, by Eric Schlosser, where he visits a facility where scientists referred to as 'flavorists' create flavours out of chemicals for fast-food producers and food manufacturers. What he found in that facility did not in any way resemble food, yet it's part of a US$1.4 billion a year food industry.

Later I conducted the same research on another packet of flavoured supposedly more healthy potato chips and find similar results with one addition that I note down in my notebook with the three letters OMG!

I find listed *mineral salt 508,* which is actually potassium chloride. It is often used as a salt substitute in reduced-salt products. The irony is that it tastes so awful they end up mixing it with regular salt for the taste. What really gets my interest though is that it is also used as an ingredient in the lethal injections for executions. Hence the OMG! Oh. My. God. Of course no one is going to die from eating a packet of potato chips but you do want to ask the question: 'Why do you have to put it in there? What is wrong with plain old salt?'

A few weeks later I find myself munching on a packet of Twisties. This is the one processed food I haven't been able to give up with my nana diet. These crunchy cheesy morsels send me straight back to my childhood and sometimes — about once a month — I just need a fix of Twisties. I put on my glasses and prepare to do another investigation, as I did with potato chips, expecting the worst.

By now I'm starting to recognise a few of the codes such

as 621 for MSG and 330 for citric acid. I am delighted to find that despite having 19 ingredients, 18 of them are naturally derived with my only concern being the aforementioned potassium chloride and the oil preserver TBHQ. It would appear that the yellow tick on the front and the words 'no artificial flavours or colours' is pretty accurate and I will continue to have my Twisties treats occasionally, empowered by the knowledge that I have checked them out.

I think I have just proven that anything with more than five ingredients is over-processed and therefore it is probably better for you to pick the one with three ingredients over the one with 28.

The yoghurt I buy is unsweetened and has listed skim milk, milk solids and cultures (including lactobacillus acidophilus). The cheese I buy has listed pasteurised milk, salt, cultures, rennet. The bread I buy has listed water, wheat flour, kibbled soy, linseed, wheat gluten, kibbled wheat, baker's yeast, vegetable oil, vinegar, salt, cultured whey, folic acid.

Now that is more than five ingredients, but I know what they all are and so would my nana, so I'm going to eat it.

These days Pearl is the reason processed foods arrive in our house. I don't stop her drinking or eating food she wants to try. Usually she's seen something advertised on television or a friend has had it at her house or in her school lunch. I don't see much point in making a huge drama out of every piece of food, and usually, because she is surrounded by so much good, nutritious and tasty food she eats more of that than junk food. I do try to educate her about reading labels and I point out, from time to time, what is in the processed food she is eating. She listens to me and that's all I expect.

After raising our five children I know that the surest

way to ensure a kid really wants to eat something is to say they can't. The minute you make it a non-issue they lose interest and make their choices based on taste rather than attention seeking.

I get a lot of slack from my family and friends about my nana diet. They point out that Nana wouldn't know what an avocado is, or a paw paw or sushi or most ethnic foods. All healthy foods. To that I say, of course, but I have a brain and the point is that by asking myself, 'Would Nana recognise this food?' I am filtering out things like foods created in a laboratory by some multi-national cashing in on reducing fat or sugar for 'healthy' eating. The jury is out on artificial sweetener but I won't go near it. For a start it tastes like poison and that's enough for me.

Studies have shown that people wanting to lose weight by swapping to 'diet' drinks loaded with artificial sweeteners, don't lose weight. No one is sure why, but that is the sad fact. If you are watching calories then a good natural option is using stevia instead of sugar.

I use it in my tooth powder recipe because I found some Japanese research that showed it can help fight dental disease. Combine that with baking soda — which has highly alkaline properties and therefore neutralises plaque acids and eliminates bacteria that cause tooth decay — and you have a pretty fine teeth cleaner. Baking soda also helps stop the major cause of tooth loss which is gum infection and inflammation. My tooth powder stops me using something which has unrecognisable ingredients on its label and it is so Nana, it's 10 out of 10. When I was a child and we ran out of toothpaste Dad would tell us to use salt or baking soda. All my tooth powder has in it is baking soda, stevia, a few drops of essential oil and I can guarantee your mouth will never feel fresher.

Why not put this book down and go have a look at the toothpaste you are using. I looked at one I bought while travelling in the United States and it had a warning which said: 'If more than used for brushing is accidentally swallowed, get medical help or contact a Poison Control Centre right away.'

In my opinion, low-fat products require some caution. These are often so highly processed to rid them of the fat, that many nutrients are lost in the process. In the worst cases, very little of the original food remains, so flavours are synthetically added.

Now I can hear you agreeing with my husband about me being a nutrition bore, so I'll stop. But not before I put in a plea about meat. In New Zealand free-range chicken and pork are readily available so please buy them if you can. It costs a little more, but you can eat less of it knowing that you are giving yourself and your family the best nutrition you can and you are also opting out of factory farming of hens and pigs, which still goes on in this country. If no one buys the factory-farmed products, they will stop being produced.

We buy free-range pork loin and make our own bacon out of it. I learned how to do this from my brother Mark, who is a chef amongst other things. He has always been a fabulous cook, even when we were children and used to take turns making our parents breakfast in bed on Sundays. (I'm still not sure how they got us to do that.) He would make the most delicious scrambled eggs and I still use his secret recipe which involves the addition of a few bits and pieces you wouldn't dream of adding. He can make ordinary old fish taste like crayfish and he taught me how to cook steak properly.

While I am always coming up with cleaning and beauty recipes, he's always experimenting with food, which is how his bacon recipe was invented. The advantage of making your own bacon is that you are not consuming nitrates, added water, colouring and chemical smoke flavour. My brother has a great sense of humour and tried to convince me to take the bacon process one step further by placing a whole leg of pork in a wooden crate packed with salt.

'Just put it down in your basement for about seven months and you should get a ham at the end of it,' he said casually.

'I don't think so,' I replied imagining rats and rotting meat.

'It'll work. That's how they used to keep meat on the ships when they sailed in the old days. Try it if you don't believe me.'

'Maybe.'

'You might want to make sure you have something underneath to catch all the drips,' he chuckled.

That was it for me. I have yet to try making ham.

Beef in this country is grass-fed so we are lucky that we are not having to buy the grain-fed, factory-farmed offerings they produce overseas, although as I write there are some applications being prepared to start factory farming in the South Island. The only thing you need to know about this is that cows' stomachs are not designed to process grain, which is their main source of food in factory farming. The rumen (stomach) contains all the right bacteria and enzymes to digest grass, because that is what they are designed to eat. If you start feeding them nothing but grain they will get sick, not sick enough to die, but they will struggle to digest it and will be susceptible to disease, which is fixed by adding antibiotics to the feed. Then there is the simply humane requirement that a cow should be allowed to graze outside in the sun, not cooped up in cubicles in a stinking shed.

In the future we should be able to buy meat and tell by its

packaging exactly where it was grown, what it was fed on, how it was slaughtered and how far it has travelled. Information I feel we are entitled to as a careful consumer. There is even a suggestion that one day we will be able to hold a barcode up to a screen, as we can do in some large department stores to check a price, and see all the information we need, including photos of the farm where it came from and how it was killed. Until then, we need to keep opting out if meat is packaged without the information we need.

And now I'll stop. But if anything I have said here strikes a chord with you, do get Michael Pollan's books – there's a list of suggested reading on page 289 – read them and take control of what you are asking your body to fuel itself and heal itself with.

The good news is that living in New Zealand means we are already free of many additives and processed foods which are standard fare in the United States. The everyday flour that we buy at the supermarket is unbleached and has no additives, most of our foods contain cane sugar rather than offloaded high-fructose corn syrup, and while our farmers and growers certainly use chemical fertilisers and pesticides, we also have a strong movement of organically-aware food producers who work hard to lobby government and prevent the worst abuses from happening. You may not be a Green Party member, but as long as the party exists we can be sure that they will act as watchdogs for any attempts at changing the food we eat. We also have a growing farmer's market culture where you can buy direct from producers and ensure you are getting the most nutritional food possible, from the closest source.

If you're reading this book you are probably, like me, a LOHAS, which has nothing to do with Lindsay Lohan. LOHAS describes people who want lifestyles of health and sustainability. We are well-educated and demand answers from manufacturers about what is going into our products and we care deeply about the environment. We have a lot of swing when it comes to the marketing and the pick-up of supposedly green products. Oh and lots of us drive a Prius!

Harness the power you have as a consumer and realise that every decision you make at the supermarket has an effect on some database somewhere. If no one bought factory-farmed pork, the farms would be closed down pretty swiftly. For more information about the consumer power of LOHAS go to www.lohas.com.

Some people have pointed out that eating like Nana used to would surely result in us all being the size of a house because of all the home-baking, the cakes, puddings and fatty roasts. To them I say take a look at the photos of your nana, or your great-grandmother and their families. There was the odd stout looking woman but not the obesity that has become commonplace now. Here are the reasons why Nana didn't get fat:

1. She wasn't drinking fruit juices laden with added sugar. Nor was she drinking a bottle of wine a night. If Nana drank, it was usually the odd wee sherry.
2. She ate less. Growing up during two world wars and a depression meant she knew how to make a little go a long way. A roasted leg of lamb would feed her family for at least three meals. She would make shepherd's pie the next night and then boil up the bones for soup the next night, adding whole grains and pulses like barley, lentils and split peas to make it go further. There were no second helpings and leftovers were recycled into another meal.
3. All her food was from her garden or somewhere close by. People had a wonderful tradition of sending beans

over the fence to their neighbours when they had too
many and receiving a cabbage back. She bought meat
from the local butcher and bread from the local baker
if she didn't bake it herself. The raw ingredients were
unprocessed and had few additives such as extra sugar
or flavourings. The quality of food was better, therefore
more filling and nutritious.

4. Nana was fit. She gardened, she swept, she bashed rugs
on the line, she hand-wrung the washing, she walked
down the road to see friends, and she didn't have a car.

5. She knew what a wholegrain was. She often baked
using kibbled wheat and rye, made desserts out of rice,
served up porridge every morning for breakfast. And
wholegrains fill you up, so you eat less.

When we first moved into our neighbourhood in Grey Lynn
we knew few people in the street. We were surprised to find
some friends we had lost touch with lived across the road but
apart from that we did the urban thing and kept to ourselves.

That was until we had hens, and for the first time
we started living in our community like Nana did. Our
neighbours out the back peered over the fence to look at the
new arrivals and introduce themselves while they were at it.
They had lived next door for three years and we'd never said
a word to each other. They were keen on getting hens too
so we swapped stories. They had just started a big garden so
we swapped produce, shared tips and the hens often got any
produce that was past its prime lobbed over the fence for
them.

Then we met another neighbour who had built the
most incredible terraced garden on his bank out of recycled
bits and pieces. I leaned out our window one day to tell him
how great we thought it looked and it turned out he had

just recovered from cancer and was doing it to keep himself healthy in remission. He grows the most incredible chillies and sells them at farmers' markets and we often do a trade over the fence of eggs for chillies. Thanks to him I have been able to grow chillies in my garden for the first time because they are benefiting from the pollen from his crops.

Our other neighbour is a businessman and keeps a very tidy home and garden, unlike us. He showed remarkable patience and fortitude with the early raids of his garden by the hens, before he recommended a builder friend who could come around to build hen-proof fences. We now feel that on all sides we have neighbours we talk to often, trade advice and produce and they help us feel like we have a small community going.

One thing no Nana had, which we do — and I'm very grateful for them — is ethnic food shops. In Auckland we have a multitude of ethnic restaurants serving up some gorgeous Asian, Middle Eastern and European dishes using fresh ingredients, herbs and spices.

We also have shops which keep the local immigrants supplied and they are a secret garden for people like me. It was in these shops I discovered the jasmine hair oil Indian women use on their hair, rose petal powder you can use as a face mask, rosewater, which I use in a lot of my recipes, great curry powder mixes, and many exotic herbs and spices I had never heard of. Next time you are in one of these shops have a good look around and don't be afraid to ask the people who own the shop what things are. I've had some great tips and advice in the past and their prices are all very reasonable.

One thing we always do in May is make apple cider. My son and his wife have an amazing old tree in their back garden which produces old-fashioned cooking apples. We gather these up, throw in some lemon and crushed ginger and a few handfuls of crab apples which grow on two trees just around the corner from us, and we bottle it up. And this is where patience comes in again. We opened our first few bottles a few months after we put them down and while they tasted gorgeous, they were really just fizzy apple juice. After a year, however, the cider tasted incredible, a hint of lemon, not too sweet and was highly intoxicating. We worked out that it's best not to touch it for at least 12 months, even longer if you can stand it.

May is also the month when my book *Domestic Goddess on a Budget* was launched. It has since sold 5000 copies. It's is the fourth book I have written — I still have a completed novel sitting in my top drawer waiting for me to do something about getting it published — and it's my favourite. I love the fact that all the recipes for cleaning products and beauty products were taken from old books, and that I tried and tested every single one of them. I wanted it to have a more green emphasis but the publishers said they had another book coming out like that so to take the green away. As far as I know the other book never emerged.

The book's publisher decided not to reprint it. I was disappointed that they didn't see the demand for the book that I could see. When stock ran out in shops and I started getting emails from people asking me where they could get it, I ordered my own reprint and started selling it on TradeMe and my website. When you write a book you become as attached to it almost as if it were a child. I encourage any author to work hard at selling your book yourself as you're the one who knows it best.

Once people could find *Dom God*, as I started calling it, we got a lot of orders and I felt that it was a book being well used. For all the book's success and popularity and the number of readers who emailed me enthusiastically to say they were making their own cleaning products and their allergies had stopped, I got a strong feeling that the busy, professional women I knew in the media just weren't getting it. Pretty soon I realised that not all women had the time to make products themselves even though they loved the idea.

'Make them yourself,' suggested Paul. 'Bottle them up and sell them.'

'No way,' I said. 'I am no business woman, it would all end in tears.'

'You never know it might take off,' he tried again.

'Forget it.'

And that was that. End of subject. Little did I know that a few months later a long lunch with a dear friend would change all that.

Easy changes you can make to eat like a nana

- Swap white rice for brown rice.
- Swap white bread for brown bread with grains in it.
- Swap anything made in a laboratory for a natural product i.e. margarine for butter.
- Eat fish twice a week. Even mullet tastes great if smoked or grilled and tinned salmon and tuna make fabulous fish cakes.
- Buy fruit fresh and often from a local greengrocer — not a supermarket.
- Shop every few days and buy just what you need. Not once a week when food is bought but often thrown out.
- Make the most of leftovers in pies, sandwiches and soups. Don't just feed them to the dog.
- Talk to your neighbours and swap produce or start a community garden. Don't just nod politely every time you see them.
- Walk everywhere you can, drive only sometimes.
- Use baking soda and vinegar to clean your house instead of buying bottles full of chemicals.
- Harness the energy of the sun to dry clothes, sell your clothes dryer.
- Make the most of seasonal fruit and veges at good prices to bottle or freeze, instead of buying tinned fruit or paying good money for out of season fruit flown in from the United States.

Food Additives

These are the main things to look out for when reading labels of the food your children eat:

- Preservatives. Sulphur dioxide and sulphites are common preservatives in dried fruit, preserved meats, some biscuits and fruit juices. Sulphites have been linked to severe asthma attacks and also stomach problems. They will be listed on the label as anything from sodium sulphite to calcium sulphite or potassium sulphite. The numbers to look out for are 220 to 228. Choose foods that have no preservatives, but be aware that their shelf life will be reduced.

- Nitrates and nitrites. These are found in virtually all cooked and cured meat, sausages, bacon, ham, frankfurters, hot dogs, salami, corned beef, pate and luncheon sausage, and may also be used in fresh meat and chicken that has been prepared in some way for sale. Nitrites are heavily restricted in some European countries. They are not permitted in organic foods in New Zealand. Try to reduce your child's consumption of smoked, cured and processed meat products, such as bacon and sausages, and look out for preservative-free labelled products or organic products. The numbers to look out for on labels are 249 to 252.

- Benzoates. These are tasteless and odourless and can be found used as a preservative in fruit juice, soft drinks, cordials and jams and chutneys. They can provoke allergy and intolerance in some people, especially those who suffer from asthma or hyperactivity. Look out for numbers 210 to 213, 216 and 218 and try to purchase products labelled as preservative free.

- Antioxidants. While natural antioxidants are great, the ones with the numbers 320 and 321 are used in oils and

fats to stop them going rancid and to stop food going
brown or developing black spots. They have been linked
to hyperactivity and allergic reactions such as rashes
and asthma and the Japanese government banned them
after a study found they caused cancerous tumours in
the stomachs of rats and mice. Use products labelled
'no artificial antioxidants', use good quality vegetable
oils like extra virgin olive oil which contain natural
antioxidants and eat fresh produce that doesn't need
additives.

- Food Colouring. Coloured foods tend to be marketed
  at children. There are 10 food colourings allowed
  into New Zealand food that health campaigners advise
  parents to avoid because of links to a wide range of
  allergic reactions including asthma, hyperactivity and
  skin rashes. They are numbered 102, 110, 122, 123,
  124, 129, 133, 142, 151, and 155.
- Artificial sweeteners. The use of saccharin and
  aspartame is common in many soft drinks, lollies and
  desserts. Their use is the subject of much controversy
  which you can view by typing their names into Google.
  But arguments aside, why would let your child eat
  something artificial when natural sugar products are
  available? Look for the numbers 950 to 955 and
  use natural sweeteners, such as honey or sugar, in
  moderation. If weight loss is necessary a natural low-
  calorie alternative is the now readily available stevia.
- Caffeine. Children are particularly sensitive to
  caffeine and can become hyperactive, nervous and have
  difficulty sleeping. Caffeine affects the nervous system
  and some scientists are concerned that brain growth
  and development may be affected in children who
  consume too much. Caffeine is present in many soft

drinks and energy drinks and children drinking several of these products could easily consume the equivalent of four to six cups of coffee a day. Check all labels of drinks you purchase for your child.

Home-made Bacon

1 free-range pork loin (you will often find it rolled
and tied with string so cut it free and spread the
loin out.)

sea salt, we use our herbed salt (see page 74)

Take the pork and slit the fat on the top with several deep gashes. Get the salt and pat it all over the meat so all sides are well covered. Place it in a plastic container with an upturned saucer in the bottom so that the meat doesn't sit in the juice that will drain out of it. (We found a great Tupperware container with a grid in the bottom of the container.) Put the lid on and place in the fridge. Check each day and drain any fluid that is sitting in the bottom. By day four it should be quite dry and ready to be sliced and fried. If you want you can smoke it at this stage for an even tastier bacon.

Apple Cider

1.5 kilograms cooking apples (these must be sour old-fashioned apples

which can only be used for cooking such as Ballarat or Granny Smith.

Look around your neighbourhood for old trees)

7 litres water

1kg sugar

3 big lemons

1 thumb sized piece of ginger, which you have squashed with a hammer

Freeze the apples for three days. Take them out of the
freezer and let them defrost. Cut them up in your food
processor including skin and core. Put in a large bucket
and pour on the cold water.

Leave for 7 days covered and stir twice a day. Strain
through a piece of muslin, old tea towel or net curtain
and mix the liquid with the sugar, grated lemon rind,
piece of ginger and strained lemon juice. Leave for a
further 24 hours.

Strain and bottle. We use old plastic bottles which
have a bit of give in them as this mixture does expand.
Leave in a cool, dark place for as long as you can.
It's drinkable after a month or so, but much more
alcoholic after a year.

Tooth Powder

Cinnamon

Mix 2 tablespoons of baking soda with ½ teaspoon of cinnamon and ¼ teaspoon of stevia powder. Put in a jar with a lid and shake up. To use, damp your toothbrush with water than stick it in the jar to get a good coating. Scrub away. Over time you will work out how much you like to use but usually a healthy covering of the brush will suffice.

Peppermint

As above but replace cinnamon with 3 drops of peppermint essential oil.

Lemon

As above but use 3 drops of lemon essential oil.

JUNE

I read an article by Julia Child in which she asked, 'Why is French cooking so good?' Her answer: 'It is love that makes it so.'

I think the same can be said of making bread. The mechanics of making a loaf of bread are not difficult, if you have the time to leave the dough to rise and a warm place to put it. But if you try to make a loaf when you are in a stinking bad mood, in a hurry, or feeling put upon, it always turns out to be a failure. You have to love making bread or at least know you're making it for those you love. It's one of the most ancient rituals you can perform in your own kitchen, knowing that for hundreds of years women have been doing the same thing all over the world most days.

My ritual starts with the kitchen. I usually make bread

in the morning so I'll wait until the family have cleared out for the day and the dishes have been done, leaving me a nice clear work bench. I take off my rings and place them in my little blue bowl on the windowsill, put on my apron and then on goes the music. Van Morrison is the most successful bread musician so far, closely followed by Joni Mitchell – although she's better for when I'm making preserves. You will find your favourites but remember it needs to be someone who calms your pulse and sends you into a more relaxed state than you were in when you entered the kitchen.

Preferably, for me, there will be a ray of winter sun gleaming through my kitchen window and there'll be the hungry blackbird who lives in the tree around the side of our house on the fence waiting to dive down and finish up any scraps the hens have left over from their morning feed.

I then do the yeast. I use dried yeast and always buy it in sachets which are just enough for a couple of loaves of bread. Yeast is a living organism, so you don't want it sitting around in a jar for months going off. In sachets it remains fresh and ready for you to open. I run the tap until the water is the right temperature, which is just warmer than blood temperature – you should just feel the heat when you dip your finger in it. Then I add the sugar and the yeast and set it up on the windowsill in the sun so that the sugar can wake up the yeast and the warmth can do the rest to get it fizzing.

I then reach for my bread making bowl, which is a big old earthenware darling called 'The Easimix Bowl' and made by T. G. Green and Co. Ltd, who make the popular blue and white striped Cornishware.

My bowl looks a lot like a traditional Mason Cash earthenware bowl but inside it has a wonderful bright green stripe around its perimeter and a big green polka dot. It immediately appealed to me in the antique shop where

I found it as it has pockmarks and stains from years of use by other women mixing cakes and bread. It also has a splash of white paint on its side – perhaps put there by someone's errant husband using her best bowl to mix up paint.

Into this lovely old thing goes my flour and any other ingredients then it too gets placed in the winter sunlight to warm.

When the yeast is frothy and smells like a strong beer I add it to the flour mixture and gently, always gently, knead the dough in my bowl before turning it out on to my board for further kneading. The art of kneading is something you learn with experience but to me the most important thing is that you get lost in the repetitive pushing and rolling. I push the dough away from me then roll it then push on the other side and then roll. I never hit or punch the dough, just knead and enjoy the 10 or so minutes I spend with my hands in the mix, pushing it around the board until it suddenly goes all elastic and shiny. I then wash out my Easimix with hot water to warm the bowl, dry it out, rub a bit of oil around its surface and put the dough back in it to rise.

Winter is not a great season in which to encourage bread to rise, as the dough really likes to be warm and cosy. If I have the wood burner on I will pop it in front of that, or perhaps in a strong ray of sunshine out the front on our deck, which is the only suntrap we have during the cold months. If I'm feeling especially loving towards my dough I'll fill a hot water bottle with warm water and sit the Easymix on that.

I wash up and go back to work in my office, patiently waiting the hour it will take my bread to rise. Then we usually have another kneading session and then another rise.

And then it's the oven. If I can I time the cooking of the bread to coincide with Pearl returning home from school.

'Bread!' she announces as she walks down the hall

inhaling the most comforting, cosy smell of home that she knows.

'How long?' she asks peering into the oven.

'Just a few more minutes and then you can take it out.'

Pearl knows that if your bread is cooked you can tap it on its top and it will sound hollow.

Half an hour later we sit at the kitchen table and devour hot fresh bread with butter. The rest of that loaf gets finished at dinner leaving one more loaf for breakfast the next day and for Pearl's school lunch.

I have several favourite recipes I use, which range from highly complicated and time consuming to really very easy, which is the one I've included here for you to try. I usually make the basic white which is steam baked and the wholegrain at the same time so I end up with four loaves, two of which go in the freezer. It is economical to do both at the same time as the white goes into a cold oven which heats up and then the wholegrain goes straight in afterwards. You will find that natural, homemade bread without additives or preservatives is really only good on the day it is baked, then for toast the next day and after that it's as hard as rock, so freezing is a great idea to keep extra loaves fresh. The pumpernickel is so damn easy and such a wonderful, healthy, filling loaf, great served with salmon and cream cheese or salami and pickles. I find that on any given day I'm happy to make one or all of them, depending on how much work I have on. And I find that at the end of making bread, I feel like I've had a little sleep and a foot massage and loved a little.

I learned an important thing in June. That a desire to be philanthropic is not always the best course of action. A few years ago I decided to become a celebrant so that I could conduct funerals for babies. Some might have said it was a calling, I just knew it was something I had to do. After Virginia's death in 1992 I felt that one day something from what I went through would turn itself into a way to help others. All these years later I feel that my understanding of those awful few days, when you try to cope and try to bury your child the right way, gives me an extra insight. By being a celebrant I felt that perhaps I could help other parents through those dark, misty days.

So I took myself off to Titirangi where I joined a group of middle-aged women seeking something in their life, and spent quite a few days challenging my sense of humour as people held talking sticks for too long and 'shared' intimate details I really didn't want to know about their lives. But I came out of it with a good sense of ritual and most importantly I knew how to conduct a funeral that would leave everyone feeling as though they had farewelled their loved one well. I have since done a few funerals and a few weddings, which I never intended to do, but when friends ask you can hardly say no.

My most significant funeral was the first child I buried. She had died of cancer and was aged six. Her family asked me to get involved as she was dying and it was a long six weeks culminating in a beautiful ceremony. I headed off that morning armed with a bottle of Rescue Remedy, for me and anyone else who needed it, and a big box of tissues.

What happened for those few precious hours had a profound effect because it frightened the living daylights out of me. It was a beautiful sunny afternoon, I conducted the funeral and then drove home in a daze. Paul and I went for a walk with Lila, who we were looking after for the day. I will never forget that walk, the way the sun shone, the light beaming through the leaves on the trees, the coffees we stopped to get.

'Feeling okay?' Paul asked cautiously.

'I feel like every vein in my body has been flushed out,' was all I could think to say.

'Right.'

Lila gurgled.

The experience hadn't reopened any grief issues I had personally — my course and years of counselling had made sure that I didn't do that — as the last thing you want is someone burying your child and harping on about their own tragic experience. It was just so penetratingly real, raw and it represented an area of life experience I realised I had been shielding myself from by getting out of corporate life and creating my cosy home office. I had become very good at keeping anything that could touch me deeply out of my life. So, as is so often the case, what seems like an honourable, worthy and right idea when you send off your cheque and sign up for a course, in reality can be incredibly wrong.

I haven't conducted another child's burial service since, which isn't to say I won't. My skin — and heart — just needs to get a little tougher first, and my philanthropy will have to wait.

Every June families all over New Zealand brace themselves for the onslaught of colds and flu. When my two eldest children, Daniel and Hannah, were younger a simple cold always brought on asthma attacks and we would be in the car and off to the local clinic to get them on the nebuliser. It was just something we got used to, and I would often turn up at work having spent a few hours in the middle of the night cradling a child who was struggling to breathe while nurses were kind and doctors attentive.

I started looking at alternative treatments back then in the 1980s, deeply uncomfortable that my kids were receiving daily doses of steroids to keep their asthma at bay. I figured if

I could just keep the cold bugs from coming into the house in the first place we would stay one step ahead.

My favourite immunity booster is a combination of echinacea and olive leaf extract. You can buy them combined in tablets with zinc, vitamin C and garlic, or I prefer getting both in the liquid form from a naturopath or a health store. Vitamin C is a great scavenger in the body cleaning up virus trash – you need about four doses a day of 500 mg if you are sick. Zinc can work to limit the virus multiplying and garlic is well-known as a folk medicine for just about anything that ails you.

I know there are no 'clinical studies' proving the efficacy of some of these products, but I also know that as soon as someone in my house shows any signs of sniffles, they get put on a course for two weeks and the cold will soon be over. I also drink lots of good quality orange juice if I am feeling poorly and limit anything that I know I have slight allergies to, such as dairy products, and drink lots of chicken soup, a folk cure used since the twelfth century, which actually does have a study supporting its healing properties. Researcher Dr Stephen Rennard at the University of Nebraska found that the ingredients can prompt a flu-fighting reaction in the body.

If you do any research into both echinacea and olive leaf extract you will find many differing opinions. I believe it is unlikely you will ever find an endorsement by any official agency because of the power of drug companies who stand to lose millions if everyone stops getting flu vaccinations, or needing antibiotics and cough and cold medications. Imagine a world where everyone fed their immune system with good quality food, regular exercise, less stress and a few herbs and hardly ever had to go to the doctor to get a prescription?

I regard the body's immune system as a big bucket. As your body fills up with chemicals and toxins from the food you eat, cleaners you spray and beauty products you put on your skin, the bucket fills up. And then your body must go to work to clean it out bit by bit to get it back down to empty again.

If your bucket is nearly full to the top because you just love that processed food, those cleaning chemicals, those fullerenes in your face cream and those dairy products to which you have a sensitivity, then when a bug does comes along, requiring the attention of your immune system, it's a bit busy and your bug might have to wait in line — a bit like turning up at Accident and Emergency at the hospital while the urgent cases get seen first.

Since I started ensuring my bucket was as empty as I could get it by rejecting chemicals in my life, I've had four years (touch wood) of a few sniffles which lasted a few days, one rather dramatic tummy bug which lasted two days and the nagging breast infection I mentioned earlier which disappeared a year after my newfound chemical free status. My family have been even healthier. Instead of regarding winter with the dread pharmaceutical companies promote through television advertising, I regard it as a perfectly normal season we experience every year. I prefer to just get my body in order and know that my immune system will take care of things.

During the winter, I always grow some broccoli, cabbage and silverbeet, because veges can be expensive and good ones are hard to come by during the winter. Where I live you can also grow lettuce right through the year, especially two particularly hardy varieties that not only thrive during the cold weather but are much better for you because they normally grow wild. Purslane (known here as miner's lettuce) and lamb's lettuce are both wild greens or weeds, which means they are more bitter than their sweeter cousins, the iceberg and cos, which have been bred and cultivated by humans to eat for hundreds of years. Because these two have had to defend themselves against predators and disease with no help from human hands, they have more omega-3 content and higher levels of phytochemicals. Nutritionally you get more bang for your buck growing them than the pretty, domesticated frilly lettuces you find in garden centres or buy at the supermarket – and they are incredibly easy to grow. You will need to buy seeds – try www.kingsseeds.co.nz – as you are unlikely to find them at your local garden centre, but I recommend you give them a go during winter to get the best nutrition you can.

A really easy way to boost your intake of greens is to grow sprouts. I know you are now thinking of mad hippies in house buses. And I'm with you on that, but those hippies in house buses know a lot about cheap, easy to grow nutrition. Initially I started growing sprouts because I had read that in order to make your hens' egg yolks that lovely rich sunflower yellow you should feed them alfalfa. Apparently, you can also feed them vegetable curry and the next day's eggs will taste of curried egg, but I haven't tried that yet.

What I did try is sprouting – something I haven't seen done since the 1970s when every house in my inner city suburb sported an old Agee jar on the windowsill with various seeds sending forth hopeful nutritious green shoots.

Paul finds them creepy. He has a phobia about plants which grow too fast ever since he read *The Day of the Triffids* as a child. He gets spooked by house plants, so we have none – except the gorgeous maidenhair I recently acquired, which lives in the bathroom. To this day I have never seen him turn his back on it.

'Nothing should grow that fast,' he commented on seeing that my alfalfa sprouts were going great guns.

But the hens love them – more than raisins, their former favourite treat, more than leaping fences, more than raiding gardens, more than shifting themselves out of the henhouse to lay their eggs. They are completely and utterly satisfied after a feed of alfalfa, a bit like me after a session with a king size bar of fruit and nut chocolate.

The eggs, well, they are simply superb. Sitting up high in the pan, blinding us with their yellow yolks, full of alfalfa goodness.

And then we started using sprouts in sandwiches, adding them to soups and stir fries, getting the benefit of their nutrition. Sprouts are so full of goodness because they represent the point of greatest vitality in the life cycle of a plant. The sprouting process pre-digests the nutrients of the seed, making it easier for us to metabolise them. Alfalfa is considered the most nutritionally concentrated of all sprouts with protein, carotene, calcium, iron, magnesium, potassium, phosphorous, sodium, sulphur, silicon, chlorine, cobalt, zinc and vitamin K, and abundant chlorophyll. And they take just a few days to make.

The start of winter is always about clothes for Pearl. Like the other kids used to, she gets a budget to spend at the start of each season and from that she must get all she needs. She usually approaches this with many research trips into town where she compiles lists and prices, brings it home, rewrites it, sleeps on it, cuts out pictures of clothes similar to the ones she wants to buy and then presents the whole lot to me in a pretty impressive presentation. All that's missing is the PowerPoint. I give it the all clear and then we drive into town and get the whole lot bought in about half an hour. That's what I call a successful shopping trip.

My wardrobe is not so easy to assemble. Since I left my corporate life I have found myself straying away from anything with shoulder pads, detailed tailoring or bought brand new. Last time I looked 90 per cent of my clothes had been bought on TradeMe or in one of the many very cool recycle boutiques in Auckland.

But before you start imagining me slobbing around in old jumpers and tweed skirts, I will have you know that most of my clothes have very expensive labels on them, representing some of the top New Zealand designers. I just never pay full price. I have constant searches in on TradeMe for my favourite designers and at the recycle boutiques I simply wander along the aisles looking for good fabrics before I bother investigating.

I am also at an age where I know what I like and what suits me, so I'm not going to be looking for the latest trendy designs. If it's black, well-designed, trousers straight-legged, skirts cut on the bias, then it's mine. I draw the line at shoes though. I have such munted feet that I need to buy very good shoes and my extravagant purchase several years ago of a pair of Venetian handmade leather boots for $800 has paid off with the boots still going strong, still in style and still worn pretty much all through winter. All I've done to them is make the luxurious addition of some possum fur insoles for added cosiness and comfort.

The secret with buying recycled clothes is to look for good fabrics and good designs. I rarely buy something which has an odour to it, but occasionally it happens. For that there is only one thing you need to do — soak it in a bucket of water in which you have dissolved half a cup of baking soda. Wash as normal and add a couple of drops of tea-tree oil to the final rinse water if you are washing by hand or a tablespoon of oil if you are using a washing machine.

I recently overheard Paul tell Pearl that I spent the least money on clothes of any woman he has ever known. I suppose that is something to be proud of, but it just made me feel like maybe I should be making more of an effort in the glamour stakes. Instead I resign myself to the fact that I work mainly from home surrounded by chickens, cats, a dog and a garden and often get quite filthy.

I once had a foot massage at an Indian beauty parlour in the neighbourhood and when the masseuse finished she clapped her hands and said: 'Feet all clean now!' with some pride. Only then did I realise that I had snuck out to the henhouse barefoot that morning to collect the eggs, which is never advisable as something always sticks.

Clothes are not the only things I acquire off TradeMe. All our kitchen crockery has come into the house in boxes full of newspaper containing two or three carefully wrapped dinner plates. I started out collecting the British Belle Fiore which is a gorgeous pattern of red and yellow flowers and then I branched out into anything British with a blue and white willow pattern. If the plates had a few chips I didn't worry because being part of our kitchen meant they'd be handled fairly roughly and I wanted my family to enjoy eating off gorgeous old plates rather than cheap ones made in China. When Paul counted more than 50 dinner plates, 30 cups and saucers, 20 bread and butter dishes and 30 pudding bowls he staged an intervention.

'You need to stop now,' he said firmly. 'We have enough.'

'But they're lovely. Everyone who comes here for a meal comments on them. They're a real taste of the past.'

'Are you planning on hosting banquets in the near future?'

'No.'

'Then why do you need so many plates?'

'Because inevitably some will break and I want to have replacements.'

'You need to stop.'

And so I did, because even I could see it was getting a little out of hand. But I just loved the act of searching, finding and bidding and I used my TradeMe sessions as a treat for when I had done a big chunk of work on the computer. I'd have a little online shopping and then get back into it.

Since then TradeMe has been responsible for most of our appliances, some lovely old pieces of Kiwiana including jewellery and my best buy so far, our three hens.

Breakfast is the meal I look forward to most. I'll often go to bed thinking about what I will make for breakfast. Will it be my cereal mix of unsweetened wholegrain muesli topped off with goji berries, a brazil nut, a tablespoon of flax-seed fibre and a swirl of homemade yoghurt? If I'm feeling virtuous and feel I need a meal with so many nutritious super foods, which is most days, I'll go for this so that I can at least know that I started the day right.

Or it might be fruit toast with homemade ricotta and the lemon curd I whip up from our eggs and lemons off the tree. Or maybe a few freshly poached eggs on some wholegrain toast with Marmite. It usually comes down to how much time I have, so if I'm in a hurry it has to be cereals. There are a few things we need from our cereals, in my opinion, for optimum nutrition. We need them to have wholegrains to provide the most nutrition and high fibre, some fruit and nuts perhaps, a bit of yoghurt or milk for a morning protein boost, and we need no added sugar. Good luck finding that.

We should aim for at least 4 grams of fibre per serving and I've seen cereals labelled as 'wholegrain' and 'source of fibre' with only 1.6 grams per serve. Distressingly our cereal manufacturers are also following the Americans in loading their product with sugar. You would think that a cereal that has on its packaging the words 'nutritious energy cereal', 'wholegrain', and 'fibre' would not be made up of nearly a third sugar. Some manufacturers have also become very clever at hiding the sugar content of their foods with words like corn syrup, cane sugar, dextrin/dextrose, lactose, maltose, honey, fruit juice concentrates, molasses, maple syrup, corn sweeteners, evaporated cane juice, malt, fructose and high fructose corn syrup.

I have only managed to find one muesli Nicolas Organic Muesli (unsweetened) on the market that isn't loaded with sugar and it has 2.3 grams per serving and that sugar comes from the dried apricots, raisins and dried apple in it. But by far the best cereal, with only 0.8 grams of sugar per serve, and nearly enough fibre at 3.3 grams is good old Weet-Bix. It seems that it really is best for Kiwi kids and adults. And then there's good old Nana porridge. If you have the time there is nothing more nutritious, low in fat, with great fibre and no added sugar. My first choice, if I have the time in winter, is a big bowl of porridge cooked with raisins or goji berries in it served with a sprinkling of chopped up nuts and yoghurt.

At one stage during my search for a decent cereal, I tried boiling up brown rice with sultanas and some spices to which I added yoghurt. It tasted quite nice and I figured I could just keep it in the fridge and scoop some into the bowl with yoghurt every morning. I lasted about three days because despite the fact that millions of people in India and Asia start their morning with rice, I just couldn't do it. In my opinion, rice is for lunch or dinner, not for breakfast.

White Bread – steam baked

This is a great economic bread to make because you put it into a cold oven. No wasting power while you wait for the oven to heat up!

25 g butter

1 tablespoon salt

1 tablespoon sugar

400 ml boiling water

1 tablespoon active dried yeast granules (not Surebake)

100 ml water — blood temperature

6 cups white flour

Put butter, salt and sugar in a large bowl and pour over boiling water. Stir until butter has melted and leave to cool to lukewarm.

Sprinkle the yeast over the lukewarm water and whisk with a fork. Set aside for 10 minutes until the yeast goes frothy.

Stir yeast mixture into the butter mixture and stir in nearly all of the flour. You should have a dough which you can knead easily and which leaves the bowl clean. Knead for 10 minutes by pushing it away from you with the heel of your hand and then rolling towards you.

Rinse your bowl out with hot water so that it heats up, dry and coat with oil then put the dough in it in a warm place for about an hour until it has doubled in size.

Push the dough down gently (don't punch) then cut in half and mould into two oval shapes. Place side by side on a greased tray and leave to rise for just five minutes, no longer. Slash the tops with five quite deep slits with a sharp knife and place on the middle rung in a cold oven. On the rung underneath place a large roasting pan which you have filled with a jug of boiling water. Close the oven door and set temperature to 200°C. Bake for 40 to 45 minutes. The loaves will be crusty and delicious.

Wholegrain Bread

It is so difficult to get a wholegrain bread that doesn't come out looking like a brick. With the extra weight of the grains it takes a special mixture to rise, and the addition of gluten flour. This recipe never fails me and I often make it at the same time as I make the white bread above. If you start preparing it once you have set the white bread dough to rise for an hour, you will be perfectly timed to pop the brown bread into the hot oven when the white bread is finished baking.

1 ½ cups kibbled whole grain (I buy this at Pak'nSave in their bulk food
    bins)

600 ml whole milk

2 tablespoons olive oil

4 tablespoons honey

3 cups white flour

3 cups wholemeal flour (use stone-ground if you can find it)

1 cup gluten flour

2 x 8 gram sachets of granulated yeast

1 teaspoon salt

½ cup linseeds (flax seeds)

Wash the grain in hot water and then put in a bowl and cover with 500 ml of the hot milk, add oil and honey. Stir to combine and leave to cool.

Leaving the remaining 100 ml of milk to cool to lukewarm, then add yeast and 1 teaspoon of honey. Leave for 10 minutes until it is frothy.

Sift flours and salt together.

Mix the yeast in with the grain and stir. Then add enough flour to make very sticky dough with a similar consistency to porridge.

Allow to rise for half an hour, covered in a warm place. Add enough of the remaining flour to make good soft dough which you can knead. You may need to add more flour than allowed in the recipe.

Knead for 10 minutes using the technique above and then shape into two loaves which you put into two greased loaf tins. Bake at 200°C for 30 minutes, or until when you tap the top gently it sounds hollow inside.

This bread freezes well.

Pumpernickel

I've adapted this from a recipe in *The New Zealand Bread Book* by Mary Browne, Helen Leach and Nancy Tichborne, which is a fantastic resource for anyone who wants to make their own bread. This is the easiest of the breads to make but the longest cooker. It is also a great way to get good wholegrains into you and the strong, malty taste goes well with fish and cheese on a platter. Always slice thinly as it is very rich and it is also great toasted. My favourite way of serving it is using a recipe given to me by my friend Niki Bezzant the editor of *Healthy Food Guide*. Mix finely chopped smoked salmon with half a cucumber peeled and diced, a little fresh ginger peeled and grated, 1 teaspoon of wasabi and 2 teaspoons of soy sauce. Serve on sliced pumpernickel.

3 cups stone-ground rye flour

1 cup kibbled rye

1 cup kibbled wheat

1 ½ teaspoons salt

2 tablespoons treacle

2 tablespoons olive oil

¼ cup bran

1 teaspoon caraway seeds

3 cups boiling water

Mix all the ingredients together in a large bowl and leave overnight, covered. In the morning add enough flour to handle the dough and shape into a loaf which you put into a well greased loaf tin, pushing down firmly and sprinkle with extra caraway seeds. Cover with foil.

Bake at 120°C for 3 ½ hours or until the loaf is firm. Take the foil off for the last 15 minutes to brown the top.

Once cooled wrap in greaseproof paper, then a layer of foil and keep in the fridge. You will need to let it sit for a day or two before you can slice it.

Breakfast Brown Rice

This makes brown rice really tasty and I often make this without the raisins to go with a curry for dinner, adding a chopped onion in when I roast the rice at the beginning. I have yet to meet a child who doesn't love it.

1 cup brown rice

1 ½ cups water

¼ teaspoon salt

¼ cup raisins

⅛ teaspoon each of ground coriander, cinnamon, ginger,

cumin and turmeric

Wash the rice and then toast it in a frying pan until it is golden brown. This gives the rice a nice nutty flavour.

Add the water and the rest of the ingredients, cover
with a lid and bring to the boil. Simmer on a low heat
for 40 or 50 minutes. Serve with yoghurt.

Making Sprouts

Buy some alfalfa sprouts from Kings Seeds (www.
kingsseeds.co.nz) or from your health shop. You can also
buy radish or onion seeds for something with a bit more
bite and mung beans for bigger sprouts to use in soups.

Place a few tablespoons of seeds in the base of a
large jar — an old Agee preserving jar is ideal — fill with
warm water and place a piece of muslin across the top
as you screw on the metal ring lid. You could also use a
sprouting lid, available at health stores. Soak the seeds
overnight and then drain all the water out. Rinse and
drain twice a day. Once they start sprouting put on the
windowsill to get some light. When they have sprouted
completely store them in the fridge for up to a week.

Home-made Yoghurt

Eating yoghurt daily, either on breakfast or made into
dips or sauces to have with curries, is a really good boost
for your health. It contains high levels of calcium and
potassium. The live bacteria in it not only aid digestion
but protect you against harmful bacteria. Unfortunately
many commercial yoghurt manufacturers heat the
yoghurt to get rid of the tart flavour and ensure a long
shelf life, which also kills the live cultures. If you buy
yoghurt check it has 'live' cultures listed on it such as
acidophilus.

To make your own yoghurt

If you can find a yoghurt maker in an op shop this makes it much easier. Basically it is an insulated container in which you place your yoghurt to culture at an even temperature for six or seven hours. Otherwise you can wrap it in blankets or towels and put it in a warm place like a hot water cupboard.

4 tablespoons live culture yoghurt — check it has live cultures such as acidophilus and is not sweetened. It should be tart tasting and might have lots of lumps in it.

900 ml warm milk — I use low fat milk.

2 tablespoons whole milk powder — this is optional but it does make the yoghurt a bit thicker

Heat the milk to scalding to kill off unwanted bacteria and then allow to cool to lukewarm. Mix in the yoghurt and the milk powder. Place in your yoghurt maker or wrap in blankets immediately. In six hours, you should have some lovely, healthy, live culture yoghurt. When you begin to run out, save 4 tablespoons of the yoghurt to use as the starter for your next batch.

Gold Potion

My potion for relief from cold symptoms tastes dreadful but definitely makes you feel better. Adding whisky makes it a little easier to get down also!

½ cup water

½ teaspoon powdered ginger

pinch cayenne pepper

1 clove garlic, crushed

1 tablespoon honey

juice of half a lemon

Boil water, ginger, cayenne, and garlic for one minute. Remove from heat and add honey and lemon juice. Cool then hold your nose, close your eyes and drink. This usually gives relief from cold symptoms for three hours.

Goji Berries

You can find these in health shops, Asian supermarkets,
where they are called Wolfberries, or at some
supermarkets in the bulk bin area. They look like red
sultanas and taste very similar, but their super food
power is incredible. They have been grown in China for
more than 600 years and they are said to enhance the
immune system, increase antioxidant levels, increase
red blood cell levels, reduce cardiovascular disease,
inhibit tumour growth, lower blood sugar levels and
reduce neuronal decline. Historically, they have
been used in China as a mild tranquilliser to relieve
insomnia, enhance weight loss, treat sexual dysfunction
and for menopause symptoms. And the good news
is you only need 10 to 15 grams a day to receive their
benefits.

Brazil Nuts

Just one Brazil nut a day is enough to raise your
selenium intake to internationally recommended levels
and eating two could lead to added health benefits. 100
grams of Brazils contain 12 grams of protein, 61 grams
of fat, 2.8 mg of iron, 180 mg of calcium and 4.2 mg
of zinc.

Flax Seed Fibre

I put flax seeds (also known as linseed) in my hen's food to give them and their eggs omega-3, but I also put the seeds in our bread. You can also buy flax seed fibre in health shops which is flax seeds ground up into a powder to put in cereal. Flax seeds are a great source of fibre. They help remove toxins from the body and regulate blood sugar, oestrogen and blood cholesterol. They also have lignans which have powerful immune boosting effects, folate, omega-3 and are rich in antioxidants. Linseed oil is not to be consumed — it is best used for oiling furniture.

JULY

As research for this book, I read through all my old columns. In doing this, I discovered that in July I always write about my birthday.

When I turned 45, for the very first time I was struck with the thought that I had at least 40 years still to go. I worked this out from the average life expectancy for a Kiwi woman, which is 81.9 and then I've added 3.1 years for recent good behaviour. It seemed like an awfully long time to fill when I've already done all the things I ever wanted to do. What will I do with those 40 years?

I had a dinner for my 45th birthday. As I looked around the table I realised that there were some people there who hadn't been at my previous birthday. There were also people who had been at my previous birthdays that weren't invited this year. Some were the same, obviously I don't go through friends quite that quickly! I also realised that none of the people sitting at the table that night had been at my 35th birthday. Age does that. It has a habit of changing your priorities.

At 45, I decided that my body had never been better. Not in a Pamela Anderson tanned and terrific way, but in a healthy way. My decision to eat only things that are created naturally has been of benefit to my body. And I realised that it's quite good to do some exercise every day.

The best thing about being 45 was turning up for a photo shoot for former editors of the *New Zealand Woman's Weekly* where I was admonished by another former editor for not following the brief of wearing 'black and white'. I hadn't read the brief. At 45 you read books, not briefs. But it didn't matter because at 45 you don't have to do white. You can do whatever the f**k you like.

A year later I found myself in the midst of a declutter nightmare. It started out reasonably enough with the alphabetising of the spice drawers and finished with the tragic sight of a middle-aged woman in her lounge winding old rags around wire coat hangers in what she thought was a uniquely creative thing to do on her 46th birthday. I especially liked the little green bows I tied to add that special home cottage flare.

What set this off was reading a book that told me my cluttered lifestyle was a result of being in denial about how much stuff I actually needed, grieving my former lives and that I had a cluttered upbringing. The last part is true so I finally get to use the 21st century's favourite justification – I blame the parents!

I called Paul from his desk, where he was trying to finish writing a book, to examine the plethora of spices and herbs which begin with the letter 'C'. He looked at the C spices, he looked at me, and without uttering a word returned to the relative comfort of his work. But my triumph was still to come – the pot cupboard re-organisation where I cleverly assigned the pot lids to their own basket.

And then came the coat hangers. I blame them on another book, which gave me the idea of spending 'many a happy hour binding them with the white waste of fabrics . . . transforming harsh wire into a chic display at no cost.' Except mine looked anything but chic. They looked like wire coat hangers with bits of old tea towels hanging off them.

I showed them off to my family at dinner. An uncomfortable silence followed.

'The pot cupboard looks great!' volunteered Hannah sensing the need to change the subject.

'Pot lid basket,' mumbled my mother to no one in particular. 'Whoever heard of such a thing?'

By the time I turned 47 things had definitely taken a turn for the worse with a visit from a poltergeist. The last time we'd had a poltergeist the whole kitchen would occasionally shake, whine and emit a high pitched scream. We were in crisis for two days as we attempted to work out what was going on. Then one of the kids finally deduced that it was the dishwasher rattling, then found a smoke alarm with a near-flat battery behind it before giving the rumbling fridge a good kick.

But for the poltergeist who visited on my birthday, there was no swift-kick solution. He was definitely a kitchen poltergeist because his influence was felt mostly in the preparation of food.

First the Bolognese sauce, from a recipe which has simmered away happily on the stove for many years without event, burned to a crisp, ruining my expensive Staub pot in the process.

Half an hour later the chocolate cake Hannah frequently bakes with much success burned dark, black and ugly.

Next my husband squirted tomato paste all over the bread and butter pudding fresh from the oven. Then I arrived in from the garden and promptly threw salad greens all over the kitchen floor. The dog lay down and leaked all over the kitchen mat (she has a condition which is normally under control), one of the cats appeared with a baby mouse in her mouth and the yoghurt propelled itself from the fridge when I opened the door, spilling its contents on the floor.

'I need a drink,' was all Paul could say. We were expecting the whole family – 22 people – for dinner.

'Get me a candle!' I shouted, to no one in particular, but Pearl came running in with a purple one. Purple is good, it represents royalty and we needed a right royal cleansing ceremony for our kitchen poltergeist.

'Salt!' I yelled.

Paul threw a bag of sea salt over to me as he reached for his second glass of wine.

'Right everyone, come into the kitchen, we're doing a cleansing.'

They all disappeared. So it was left to me to do the business, as usual. I lit the candle and said in a very firm, royal voice: 'You are not welcome here and I command you to leave.'

I heard sniggering coming from the lounge, but I ignored it, quite rightly discerning that it was my family, not the poltergeist, in stitches.

From there I sprinkled salt thoroughly and dramatically all over the kitchen, as if sowing seed in the garden. I continued my quest in every other room in the house for good measure, and made sure the sniggerers in the lounge got a good covering as well.

'That should do it,' I said, eyeing the candle whose flame had started to waver.

And then everyone arrived.

We had rescued the Bolognese with a few dollops of peanut butter, a tip I found in one of my old cookery books, thus creating an Asian-inspired Italian dish. We cut the top off the cake and iced it. We scraped the tomato paste off the pudding, picked more greens from the garden, wiped off the dog, dispensed with the mouse and let the dog eat the spilled yoghurt.

'It's very hot in here,' said my father, escaping out the kitchen doors into the freezing winter night, with the urgency of a man who has been locked in a sauna for a week.

'Hot!' said everyone else, shedding layers furiously.

The candle wavered.

Lila, our granddaughter, screamed like a banshee when we tried to put her to bed in the cot that she always sleeps in without a murmur of complaint.

The candle wavered.

'That's it,' I announced to our dinner guests. 'Open all the windows and doors and make lots of noise.'

It was my birthday. I had just turned 47. I was obviously senile already.

They all sang 'Happy Birthday' and the girls screamed at the end for good measure.

And then it was all over.

A strange calm descended on the kitchen, everyone left, the windows and doors were closed and I blew out the candle.

'That feels better,' said Paul settling down on the couch with yet another glass of wine even though he looked like he really didn't need another one.

I wondered what would happen at my 48th birthday. I have yet to find out, but I'm pretty sure there will be something hilarious or quirky to write about next year because July is just that sort of month.

We're enjoying the log fires and the cosy nights but short days always bring about a stroke of boredom with me and when I get bored, watch out.

This winter our cosy fires are being fuelled by newspaper bricks. Paul became a little obsessed with making newspaper bricks over the summer. If he had any spare time you could always find him at the kitchen table ripping up old newspaper into strips. I sometimes had to remind him to stop doing it if we had visitors as he seemed to think it was perfectly alright to rip away while having a conversation. I bought him an electric shredder but he was having none of it.

'They work better if it's done by hand,' he said in a gnarly old voice. 'Best not to cut corners with the brick making.'

Initially, he hadn't been so keen when I ordered a brick-making device off the internet.

'It's a great way to recycle,' I said enthusiastically.

We worked out what to do and made about 10 drab looking wet lumps of papier maché.

Paul refused to let me dry them out on the front veranda, where there's usually washing hanging and the odd chicken floating around.

'We already look like mad hippies, they can dry downstairs,' he said firmly.

He then pointed out that if I read the instructions I would know not to use glossy paper in my bricks – I had presumed all paper was alike.

'You do it then,' was all I said and Paul soon found the same contentment and Zen-like quality I find in making bread, by making newspaper bricks.

He disappeared for half an hour and emerged with 20 lovely looking bricks of paper. Now we just had to wait for them to dry for a few weeks and apparently they would burn, with wood, for a couple of hours. Our first test batch burned a treat and we now have about 200 of them lovingly and aesthetically stacked against the fence, covered with a tarpaulin so they dry out over summer and stay dry in winter.

Paul is also the only one who can roast the coffee beans in our house. We must have saved hundreds of dollars over the two years he has been buying green beans online and roasting them on the stove in a frying pan. The only time I have tasted better coffee was when we were in Mexico, where I became so addicted to the local coffee that I filled a suitcase with the stuff to bring home.

Coffee so often gets a bad rap with conflicting studies coming out every month. If you type 'coffee health facts' into Google you will get 1.28 million responses. Coffee has been used for hundreds of years by people wanting a stimulant. In folk medicine it was used to treat snakebites, asthma and headaches. The reason it is offered at the end of a meal is to stimulate digestion and it also purges the bowels for people prone to constipation. You can also use the wet grounds as a poultice for bruises and insect stings.

I drink one cup a day to get me kick started as I sit down at my computer, so I make sure it's the best cup it can be both in terms of how it was grown (sustainably and fairly traded, free of chemicals such as a herbicide and pesticide sprays) and in terms of taste. By the way, if you drink decaffeinated or instant coffee, do be aware that petroleum-based solvents and other chemicals are often used in their manufacture.

We make our coffee using a moka pot, which Italians use to make espresso coffee at home. I find it makes a perfect cup compared to the expensive espresso machines some people have in their homes.

When I came back from visiting Morocco, I began to make the Turkish-style coffee that is commonly served there.

It is a delightfully spicy, sweet, short kick of coffee. You can get it made beautifully in some restaurants but I love making it myself. The hard part is finding the very finely-ground, almost powdery coffee, which most home grinders, including mine, won't be able to grind fine enough. Thankfully, you can usually buy it at Middle Eastern food shops or online. The combination of cardamom with the sugar and coffee is divine and I often make this at the end of a dinner party for my guests. I serve it in tiny demitasse cups and remind them not to drink the grounds!

Winter always brings out the urge to cook big nourishing stews and casseroles. I used to enjoy using a slow cooker to make them when I was going out to work, because I could put it on in the morning and come home to a house full of lovely smells and a tasty casserole at the end of the day. But now I turn to my trusty old pressure cooker that I spied during one of my op-shop hunts. It was a Presto 406 and it still had its handbook inside, so I figured I could work out what to do with it when I got home. I came into the house holding it out in front of me beaming with pride.

'Have you forgotten what they do?' whispered Paul with such fear and loathing that I could only presume he was having a particularly nasty childhood flashback involving the worst kind of suffering.

That turned out to be largely true. We both grew up with mothers who pressure cooked and we both have memories of loud screeching coming from the kitchen as the indicator weight on top of the cooker fired into the roof of the kitchen with the ferocity of a moon launch, due to some pressure mishap.

Then there was the food – odd concoctions involving tripe, mutton and hearts.

On opening my instruction booklet, there they were —
the recipes for stewed tripe, boiled knuckle of mutton and
stuffed hearts. Neither of us can quite remember forcing our
fussy appetites through creamed calf's head but it was nice to
see we had the recipe for that too.

'I'm not eating anything which comes out of that,' Paul
announced before stomping off to get Marigold, the naughty
hen, out of my lettuce patch.

'It only takes 20 minutes to cook beef curry!' I shouted
after him. 'And 15 minutes for a small chicken!'

'Not listening,' he mumbled.

'This masterpiece of cast aluminium is the new
microwave,' I informed him with authority, forgetting that the
pressure cooker came first. 'And it keeps all the vitamins and
nutrients in the food, not to mention phyto-somethings in
vegetables.'

'Shut up.'

The next day I announced the great pressure-cooker
experiment. I would buy the cheapest beef I could find and
cook it. The proof would be in the eating, judged by my
family.

'Can you at least get it from the organic butcher?' Paul
pleaded.

'Not on your life,' I shouted as I left the house. 'It'll be
one of those butchers with the big red signs and ads for $10
meat packs for us.'

All went well as I spent half an hour reading the
instructions and marvelled at the technical mind of the '50s
housewife, able to decipher such words as 'vent pipe' and 'over-
pressure plug'. Within moments I had assembled a beef curry
featuring dirt cheap chuck steak, and onto the stove it went.

Something went horribly wrong. Steam started escaping
from underneath the lid.

'It's not supposed to do that,' said Paul, suddenly interested now that the great experiment was a sure disaster.

'Get out of my kitchen!' I shouted, wondering why I was suddenly sounding like my mother.

In the booklet, I found the page called 'Reversing Sealing Gasket,' followed the highly technical instructions and then couldn't get the lid back on. I jumped up and down on it, I sat on it.

Pearl wandered in as I was attempting to hit it with a hammer and innocently inquired: 'What are you doing?'

'Get out of my kitchen!' shouted my mother's voice.

Time was running out. I only had 20 minutes until dinner, I began to sweat profusely. I needed to prove that my pressure cooker not only saved money, time and energy but would also cook nutritious foods which tasted good. I was beginning to understand the term 'pressure-cooker life'.

After five minutes of head-in-the-hands mumbling at the kitchen table I realised I had put the gasket in the wrong slot.

'Honestly, this is delicious,' snorted my husband 20 minutes later, mouth bulging with melt in your mouth tender beef.

The pressure cooker experiment had paid off, and my family still demand and devour their weekly beef curry. However the pressure cooker I use isn't the same one that was such a success that night. Later that week I decided to cook a duck in it and didn't put in enough liquid. It went dry, there was this awful sound and the whole thing exploded, just like my mother's one did.

Fortunately I found exactly the same model to replace it on TradeMe and we've been great friends ever since. It cooks chickpeas and kidney beans in half the time it normally takes and turns scraggy bones and bits of barley into wonderful soups.

During the winter I find myself focusing on the birds who live on my small, urban property. Food becomes scarce during the cold months, so I decided that it was time we had a bird feeder. You can simply throw bread and scraps out on your lawn for birds, but with three cats I decided that we needed a safer delivery mechanism.

I already have a bird bath and am rewarded by the sight of blackbirds and sparrows having baths and drinking in the hot months. After a visit to the garden centre, I came home with a kitset for a bird feeder which would stand 1.5 metres off the ground, safely out of harm's way from my cats. I then spent a happy afternoon in the winter sun on the lounge floor working out how to put it together. I like to do a bit of carpentry now and then, even if my finished products have a bit of a lean to them or in the case of the window screen I made for our bedroom window, are a little small. Once I'd managed to put the bird feeder together, I put it out right in the middle of the garden so that I could see it from the kitchen. For me, part of the joy of feeding birds is being able to watch them. Onto the feeder I put out bread for the sparrows, two apple halves for the blackbirds and wax-eyes and a little bowl of lard. And then I waited. Nothing happened and then it got dark. The next day I waited again. Nothing happened and then it got dark.

'I don't think they like where you've put it,' said Paul with frustrating good sense.

'But if I put it back into the trees I won't be able to see them,' I argued.

'I thought this was about feeding the birds, not putting on a show.'

So I shifted it a metre back into the trees and had barely got back inside before what seemed like the entire bird population of Grey Lynn had descended.

I was so delighted I insisted on pointing it out to everyone who had the misfortune of stepping into my kitchen. I soon realised that the lard was actually being eaten by sparrows rather than my precious wax-eyes, so I made up a lard cake that I then suspended from a tree in an old onion bag. This makes it much easier for the wax-eyes to get to as they don't mind hovering in the air while they eat.

I still had one bird I needed to get into my garden. The native tui is a rare bird to see in the inner city but lately I've been hearing their gorgeous trilling in my neighbour's trees and occasionally they dart over my house chasing each other.

You can encourage them by planting native flax and kowhai as they feed off their flowers. You can also put out sugar water. The secret is to put it in a red bowl or cup as this apparently attracts them.

I mixed up the sugar water, found a little red plastic bowl and added it to the usual daily bird-feeder menu. After a while of waiting for a tui to turn up, I forgot about it, figuring the few tui that had made their home in my neighbourhood were being well fed elsewhere.

Then one day, as I was making the most of the winter sun and sitting out on the deck eating my lunch, I heard a familiar trill. I turned around very slowly to look at the bird feeder and there they were. A pair of tui drinking away. I crept inside as slowly and inconspicuously as I could before shouting, 'Tui, tui, quick the tui have arrived!' as if welcoming long lost relations.

Everyone kept doing what they were doing so I resumed my spot in the sun and sat solo, enjoying the company of my tui.

I then made up a seed cake to attract goldfinches and some doves I had seen flying around. By making it into a seed cake, you stop the seed scattering all over the ground and sprouting unwanted weeds. We had the occasional visit from a group of goldfinches, but two spotted doves moved in. When they weren't feeding, they perched on top of our roof and warbled that lovely soft 'cuck-oo' they make. They were by far the prettiest birds we have had in our garden, with their distinctive bands of black and white spots around their necks. They did seem rather thick though, spending far too much time for my comfort on the ground grooming and exposing themselves to feline attack.

One night we were in the lounge watching television when we heard some thumping in the kitchen. It sounded like one of the cats was having a play and bumping into the chairs, so none of us got up to investigate.

Later, when I went out to make a cup of tea I saw one of my doves, bloody, dead and lifeless in a pile of feathers on the floor. Nearby Kitty, our hunter, sat grooming herself proudly. Doves are big birds, so I couldn't fail to be a little impressed with Kitty's ability to drag it through the cat door and murder it. But from that day on I stopped putting out seed and I've never seen doves again. I figure it's safer that way.

By the end of July I have marked another birthday and usually spent a few minutes longer than I should gazing at my face in the mirror. Every woman does it, the face gymnastics where your hands pull and scrape away at your flesh, pulling it back at the cheekbones, up at the brow, imagining ourselves post-op after an age-saving facelift. And then I just accept myself for who I am, even if there is a new wrinkle on my top lip and a few bags and sags that weren't there last year.

I feel the same way about ageing as I do about size. If I meet a woman for the first time I'm interested in her smile, her eyes, and her personality. Later I might notice what size she is, and perhaps that she has a few wrinkles around her eyes, but I firmly believe that no one seriously judges someone by how they look. So I try to make sure that I'm as interesting as I can be as a person so that I can hold a decent conversation. I try to make sure that I'm happy so that I'm always smiling. And I try to live an honest life full of good karma so that you can see that behind my eyes.

Newspaper Bricks

If you're interested in buying a
briquette maker for your recycling
man and if he doesn't mind looking like a 'mad
hippy' then go to www.nznature.co.nz. Once you've
got a briquette maker, it's easy. All you do is rip old
newspapers (no gloss or photos) and throw them in
an old garbage bin to half way. Fill the rest with water,
stir occasionally and leave for a few days. Then you get
the pulp and squeeze it in the briquette maker and out
come little bricks. Now that's a great way to recycle,
right at home.

Roasting Coffee Beans

Get a large, heavy-based frying-pan and
put it on a medium heat.

Pour in a layer of green coffee beans
and let it heat up as you stir or shake the pan to get the
heat evenly distributed.

Adjust the heat if you need to, but the beans should
start turning brown fairly quickly so keep turning and
shaking. They will start to shine, which is a sign the oil
is being released, and they will smoke and you will hear
a cracking sound.

When they are mostly dark brown and the cracking
sound gets a little less frequent, tip them out on some
newspaper. They will continue to cook for a while and
then cool.

Once cool, store in an airtight container and leave
for about four days before you start using them.

Turkish Coffee

250 ml water

4 heaped teaspoons Turkish coffee

2 teaspoons caster sugar

a big pinch of ground cardamom

Put the water in a small saucepan or, if you can find one, a traditional Turkish coffee pot which has a narrow neck and is sometimes called a cezve. Add the coffee, sugar and cardamom, and slowly bring it to the boil. If you boil it too fast, you will lose some flavour. Just as it starts to boil and foam rises, take it off the heat. Do not stir at any time in the process. Wait for a few moments then put it back on the heat to get nearly to the boil and then take off. Do this once more (three times in all). You should have some froth on it (the more froth the better the coffee) and then pour it into the cups.

Pressure-cooker Beef Curry

This is a lovely old-fashioned recipe which came with the instruction manual for my old pressure cooker. Both Paul and I remember having it as kids, so might you.

1 kg chuck steak or gravy beef. Any old cut will do.

1 tablespoon olive oil (the recipe said fat but oil is easier for us to get!)

1 onion, sliced

1 apple, sliced

3 teaspoons curry powder (original says 2 teaspoons but I think we like it hotter these days)

1 teaspoon chutney

2 teaspoons lemon juice

salt

600 ml water

1 tablespoon flour

Cut the meat into small cubes. Add oil to the cooker and brown the meat. Add sliced onion, apple and curry powder and brown lightly. Add chutney, lemon juice and salt with the water. Place lid on cooker. Allow steam to flow vigorously from the vent pipe to release all air from the cooker. Place indicator weight in position and cook for 20 minutes. Thicken if necessary with corn flour.

Bird Feeding Recipes

Wax-eye Cake

Melt 1 cup of fat (lard or dripping are best). To that add 2 cups of rolled oats, 2 cups of bran, 1 cup of sugar and 5 cups of water. Pour into a roasting dish and place in freezer. As it freezes, cut it into pieces (it's impossible to cut when completely frozen). Put pieces into an onion bag and hang it in a tree where you can see it.

Tui Sugar Water

Mix 1 cupful of sugar with a litre of water. Place in a red container on a bird table or hanging from a tree, and wait for the tui to come.

Seed Cake

Simply melt some lard or dripping and pour into it some wild-bird seed you can buy at your supermarket, pet shop or bulk-bin store. Follow the directions for the wax-eye cake above for pouring and cutting.

AUGUST

In the winter the hens are supposed to stop laying, but mine didn't this year. It seems the cold and the diminished sunshine hours don't affect their mood or their ability to reproduce. I, on the other hand, go into a total decline when the cold hits my bones. And every year I find a new article of clothing, wrap myself in it and convince myself that without it I will certainly die. The first was my drab, green cardy that made me look like Miss Marple when she was knitting socks, not solving crimes. I began to talk to Drab Green Cardy which worried me for a little while, especially when I had a conversation with him about how he had to stay home while I went out to lunch.

'Please don't get me wrong, I love you, I couldn't live without you on cold mornings at my desk, but there are some places it is not safe for you to visit.'

Drab Green Cardy glared at me from the pile of clothes

in the bedroom.

'I am your muse,' he grumbled. 'I am the cloak of your creativity. Without me you are nothing.' He spat that last word, with an emphasis on the 'na' and then flinging the 'thing' in my face.

He was far too aware of my recent slip in appearance. Days spent padding around without make-up, unwashed hair and grubby slippers immersed in my new winter look he had cruelly dubbed 'rest-home chic'.

'You used to make an effort, the fine Indian cotton dresses, the gorgeous ear-rings you wore all summer which you found in that Moroccan souk,' taunted Drab Green Cardy. 'Before you let yourself go, became all reclusive and made me your fashion victim.'

'I would watch it if I were you,' I said. 'For a $20 chain-store clearance garment you have a lot of points on yourself.'

But there was some truth in what he had to say. Winter dressing leaves little to inspire a woman once you get past the enthusiasm of wearing those flattering black tights, your favourite boots and that gorgeous vintage camel coat. The rest belongs in the vague realms of layers incorporating spencers, anything with merino in it, bulky jumpers and cardies and pants that hopefully still fit after the excesses of summer.

'Quite frankly it's been a while since you wore those black pants and someone should tell you that it's been a while since you fitted them as well,' noted Drab Green Cardy.

'Now that is just being mean,' I told him.

On my return from lunch, refreshed and invigorated by my rare outing, I gratefully disrobed, eager to get back into my comfort clothes, including Drab Green Cardy.

But he was nowhere to be found. Not under the bed or on the pile of clothes on the floor. I half-heartedly looked in the wardrobe knowing full well I rarely hang clothes up, let alone cardies. I was distraught, missing his comfort and warmth, craving his funny old pockets, caring for the half-eaten biscuit I was saving for later.

'Hi, Mum,' said Pearl anxious to see what the commotion was at the end of the hall and munching a half-eaten biscuit I vaguely recognised.

And there he was. Comforting and warming my daughter.

'My cardy!' I shouted.

'Lovely isn't he,' she cooed. 'I love him,' she continued stroking his arms softly.

Drab Green Cardy was strangely silent for once, no doubt looking forward to his upcoming hip-hop class and hours spent hanging out with a bunch of 12-year-old girls and singing along to Lady Gaga.

'Keep him,' I told my daughter, hoping he was listening. 'He did nothing for me anyway. Now where is my nice Indian pashmina?'

My pashmina was brought back from India by Paul and it rarely leaves my side. It's travelled with me across the world and back five times and has learnt to bundle itself up into the smallest of handbags, ready for me whenever I feel a chill. But last winter I just needed more, and that was when I stormed out of the house and returned with the mother of all winter coats — the puffer jacket.

I'm sure there are some people who do things knowing full well that there is something deeply challenging about their actions. Something which crosses all boundaries of good taste. Something which means that when you are eventually discovered you will be forced to defend the indefensible.

Like the Tuesday morning when Paul returned home unexpectedly from work, opened the bedroom door and found me.

'What the . . .!' was all he could say.

I looked at him from what I hoped was a position of superiority and the indisputable right to be.

He turned his back.

'I hadn't realised it had got this bad,' he muttered before sitting on the end of the bed and putting his head in his hands.

'It's not my fault,' I pleaded. 'It must have something to do with the ageing process.'

But it was no use trying to justify myself. Because I was the one sitting in bed under two duvets while fully clothed in a duck-down full length puffer jacket, complete with hood. My hands were encased in merino fingerless gloves and what he didn't know was that I had the electric blanket turned on full blast and still had my ugg boots on under the duvets.

'We need to have a talk,' was all he said as he walked down to the kitchen to make coffee.

It has been a winter of humiliation for my family. While they swan around in a couple of thin layers of cotton, I am either fully encased in ugg boots and my puffer jacket, or lying in a hot bath or hugging the log burner. You will not find me in any other position.

'You used to have such style,' said Paul, pouring the coffee. 'Lovely vintage camel-hair coats, merino sweaters, cashmere scarves. Why the puffer jacket, why in bed?'

'I love him,' was my helpless response.

It all started when Alex came around in her new jacket recently bought in a sale.

'Here try it,' she said, holding it out for me.

'Oh God no, imagine me in one of those, I'd look as big as a house! They're just for skinny young people like you.'

But I tried it anyway. It was a little tight, but I got the overall feeling. It crept all over my body like a tidal wave of comfort. It was the unfamiliar sensation of warmth. The first I had felt all winter. My bones cried out, my back cried out and my brain said 'get one . . . now.'

And so my puffer jacket was purchased the next day. A larger, longer version than our daughter's but from the moment I shrugged it on, I knew we would be together for a long, cold winter even if it did add 30 kilos to my already healthy frame.

'I see you've gone for comfort this season,' said my lunch friend whose wardrobe turns its nose up at anything less than the finest labels.

'Sticks and stones to you, I'm warm and I don't care,' I responded.

'Do you ever take it off?' she inquired three hours later, aware of the looks we were getting from the other patrons.

'Not often,' I said. 'I tried wearing it to bed the other night when he wasn't looking but he was having none of it.'

Thus my secret solo morning sessions in the bedroom. No one turns heaters on in my house, preferring to exist like some rare genetic Inuit offshoots braving it out, breathing fog out of their mouths over their cereal. I refuse to get out of bed. And when they leave I jump out, grab the jacket and get back in with my laptop to work.

'It's like you have found your own individual, portable padded cell,' said Paul in the reasonable way he does when he is trying to embarrass me out of doing something.

One thing he never complains about is my addiction to baths in the winter. I'm not sure if it is because it gets me out of the way for an hour or because he can come and natter to me for an hour and have a captive audience. Either way, bath time in my house is top on the treat list and there are few activities I like more in the winter than having a nice hot bath and a good soak. Sometimes it is the only thing that can warm my bones.

This year I became a little obsessed with chlorine in the water and the fact that I was soaking in lots of it, most days. I had rigged up two 200-litre rainwater tanks to collect water out of two of our downspouts. I could work out how to run a hose into the bath, but not how to heat it. In the old days I could have run it through a califont, which I had experienced in one of my first flats. It was gas powered and sat over the bath. When you wanted hot water, you lit it, then it heated the water as it ran through. I loved it but I have no idea where I'd find one of those now.

Instead I started researching how to get rid of the chlorine in my bathwater. First I bought a shower head, manufactured here by Methven, which uses vitamin C to take out the chlorine as it comes through your shower. And then I found sodium thiosulphate, which also takes out chlorine, so I throw a teaspoon of it in every bath and I find the water is much softer and easier on my skin. It is an antidote for cyanide poisoning so I figure it's handy to have around and it's also an anti-fungal so that's good to know!

Over the years I have thrown many things into my bath to make me feel better. Rose geranium oil always goes in for pre-menstrual tension or general hormonally challenging days. Oats go in by the cupful to calm down any rashes (you do need to clear the plug before letting the water out). And my most luxurious bath involves milk, just like Cleopatra — try it once and you'll never go back (see page 24).

Taking a long hot bath is an antidote for so many things. It can act as a signal that your day has ended, provide a much needed warm-up in the middle of a winter's day, or be an indulgent soak on a Sunday afternoon. Paul tells me that I once stayed in a hot bath for three hours, although I have no recollection of ever having time for such complete indulgence. The secret to making bath time your time is to have a lock on your bathroom door, or to simply use your serious voice to instruct family members to leave you alone.

I love the Virginia Woolf quote from her book *A Room of One's Own*: 'A lock on the door means the power to think for oneself.'

Dim the lights, light a candle, bring in the portable stereo with some relaxing music – I like a bit of Bach in the bath – and away you go. Don't try to read or do a crossword, just lie back and relax. I often combine one of these sessions with a face mask and a hot-oil hair treatment. Just make sure you have a large jug filled with clean water nearby for the final hair rinse.

If I haven't got time for a bath and need a quick winter warmer I make a hot ginger drink from a Balinese recipe. It gives me a lovely warm inner glow when I have come in from the cold. I'm sure it's also very good for me too.

August was the month I discovered soap making and I have to say that I have never used a castile soap as lovely as the first batch I made. Creamy, soft and long lasting it is a great thing to be able to create, but making it for the first time was a bit scary.

I first turned to one of my old books, called *Household Discoveries,* which was published in 1909. It is written by a man called Sidney Morse and sets out its purpose in the first sentence: 'The main object of this book is economy. If rightly used, it will save a great deal of money in every household. It will also save time and labour, which are the equivalent of money.'

I have yet to read any pages of Sidney's book and not leave the room screaming. His interpretation of time and labour seem to be slightly out of skew with modern times because everything he suggests seems to take five days and several hundred hours worth of stirring over outdoor cauldrons. His advice for soap making did not disappoint. Over 13 pages of tightly packed type he fills you in on the 'domestic art of soap making' where you make your own lye by soaking wood ash in water for a hundred years, and rather distressingly eat a lot of soap.

'The best test of soap is to apply the tongue to it. If it bites the soap contains an excess of free alkali and is not suitable.'

I eventually found a recipe in one of my more modern guides to less toxic living which seemed doable by modern standards. It stated that making a batch of soap takes about the same amount of time as making bread. I make bread, so therefore I could now make soap, I reasoned.

My first problem was how to get hold of some caustic soda, also known as lye in soap-making terms. My local pharmacist promised to order some in and then rang to say it was no longer available. My local bulk food store had some out the back but my first batch was a dismal failure, due to the inability to work out just how caustic this unlabelled batch of soda was. There was nothing for it but a visit to my local hardware store where I found one hundred per cent caustic soda or sodium hydroxide marketed as a drain unblocker complete with warnings that it was highly corrosive.

'Just what part of green natural living does "highly corrosive" play?' asked the ever vigilant Paul, who had only just recovered from witnessing the highly emotional drama that had unfolded with my first, failed attempt to make soap earlier that day.

'Nature is full of naturally occurring poisons, the secret is how to manage them,' I bluffed.

And there I was. Safety goggles on, pouring water onto the caustic soda and watching it fizz and emit its highly corrosive gasses. The next problem was that I had to heat that mixture and the other mixture of olive oil, coconut oil and Kremelta (the only vegetable shortening I could find) both to 100°C before I could mix them together to saponify, or turn into soap.

'God it stinks in here,' announced Paul as I stirred and swapped my jam making thermometer from one pot to the other – note to self: splash out on another thermometer.

And it did. It smelled just like soap. A big, raw, earthy soap.

I mixed everything together, the mixture foamed, I ran outside with the pot and whisked as if my life depended on it for half an hour.

By which time I didn't care if it worked or not. I was completely over it, but still cautiously wearing my safety goggles.

Luckily Paul reminded me that a job well done is one which is finished – no doubt having flashbacks to a recent event where a gathering of half-finished curtains lay discarded on the kitchen table for three months waiting for me to hem them.

And so I threw in some lavender oil, poured it all into Tupperware containers and left them outside, ignored, for a few days.

'Who made the soap outside?' asked Daniel when he popped around for coffee.

'Oh those,' I said. 'Don't think they worked. Bloody nightmare.'

He opened a lid and peered inside.

'Looks like soap to me.'

And it was. Creamy, nice smelling castile soap which was lovingly dried for four weeks and was often brought out, like a brand new white, fluffy kitten, to be shown proudly to visitors.

It would be months before I would be brave enough to make another batch, but I'm glad I did. I bought a new thermometer for the occasion and on re-reading the recipe discovered that I wasn't actually supposed to bring everything up to the boiling point of 100°C, but the slightly less bubbly and scary 100°F. This discovery made the second session so much less dramatic. I did learn something though.

My first batch, which still remains as the best ever, used very basic ingredients. Rough old coconut oil I had bought from an Indian shop, cheap olive oil from my large tin which I cook with and Kremelta off the supermarket shelves. For my next batch I bought refined coconut oil and vegetable shortening, and it wasn't nearly as nice. It just goes to show that sometimes the best stuff comes off your kitchen shelves.

I have since found out that Paul's concerns about the use of drain cleaner were unnecessary. The chemical reaction that takes place during the saponification of the oil releases any caustic or damaging elements in it.

You can have a lot of fun with soap making. You can play around with different oils, throwing in almond or avocado oil for a really special soap, and you can add colouring and different essential oils to make them smell gorgeous. Some people also add very fine clay, or seeds to get a scouring effect when the soap is used. I prefer just the good old white soap, slightly scented with lavender oil.

On 28 August, I set off to have lunch with one of the busiest women I know, Auckland's PR queen Deborah Pead. Deborah and I should never technically be friends because she's quite right and I'm quite left when it comes to politics but there is no one I enjoy arguing with more. And she is very different to me because she is always 'on' whereas I am quite often 'paused' or 'off'. She is always on the job, and that is why she is a great

PR woman. She will arrive with a goody bag full of her clients' products for me, and within five minutes of sitting down at lunch she will manage to drop about half her client's names and products into the conversation and after 20 minutes she will have mentioned them all. That's when I know we can start to really talk. That and the fact that I've poured two glasses of wine into her. This lunch was a long overdue catch up, and if I'm honest I was a bit down in the mouth.

'I hear something's up,' said Deborah in her matter of fact tone.

'Like what?' I said hedging.

'Tell me you are not going to go back into magazines. Tell me you are not going to get all corporate again, after everything you've done to shape your life. Your wonderful life, I am always so damn jealous of your life!' she said. Deborah is South African but she actually talks like an Italian a lot of the time, full of passion and ebullience.

She was referring to the fact that I had been seeing a bit of my old boss from my days editing magazines. There was an editing job up. I had been thinking about it and I had mentioned my interest to him.

'Yes, yes, I know what you are talking about,' I snapped back rather hastily. 'But tell me this, Deborah. I am bored shitless with my wonderful life. I can't spend the rest of my life writing books, tending chickens and playing with baking soda and vinegar.'

'Oh and now you are being ridiculous,' she tut-tutted.

What I didn't tell her was that I had spent two weeks winding myself up into a frenzy about whether I should step back into the editing chair, only to find that my old boss had found someone else more suitable than Old Faithful.

'I'll tell you what you are to do,' said Deborah filling my glass. 'You have this marvellous thing happening, this Green

Goddess, all these women making your cleaners and getting rid of the chemicals. But can I be honest with you, Wendyl?' she said, leaning in close. 'I love the idea, but I would never have the time to make the damn things. So make them. Make them for women like me who want to be goddesses, but don't have any damn time.'

I laughed. And then I laughed again. I am no entrepreneur. And I told her so.

'I can't even keep track of the business I have writing stuff for very regular payers. I have no desire to start a company, or be in manufacturing or retail so let that be an end to it,' I said firmly shutting her up. Or so I thought.

While I was upstairs paying a visit to the ladies, Deborah rang Paul and suggested he might like to join us for a late afternoon glass of wine.

I think he must have flown the two kilometres from Grey Lynn to Ponsonby because he was there within moments and listening eagerly to Deborah's latest idea. Let me just say here that Deborah has some of the best ideas in Auckland, for which she earns a great deal of money from very important business people, so to have her sitting at my table offering them for nothing, and having me rudely laugh my head off, might have been a little odd for her.

But Paul didn't laugh.

'I love it,' he said, eyes sparkling.

'Here, take a look at this,' said Deborah pushing across the table notes she had been scribbling on some paper she had found in her bag earlier in the lunch. At the top of the page were the words 'Boredom Buster!' and she had scribbled words like 'empowerment of women' and 'sustainability' and most importantly 'the range'.

I know what she wrote on that piece of paper because she made me take it home with me where it sat, unloved, and discarded at the bottom of my purse for weeks.

We talked for an hour longer and slowly I realised that Wendyl's Green Goddess could happen, but only if Paul made it. He had run a successful knitwear business with his ex-wife in the '80s and, unlike me, he had the skills required.

The next day a PR guy for The Home Show, Paul Blomfield, rang me to see if I would give a talk at the show about natural cleaners and living like a nana. A light went on in my head.

'I'd love to, but could I also set up a table and sell my new range of cleaners?'

'I didn't know you had a range of cleaners,' he replied.

'Neither did I until now.'

'Oh well . . . of course,' he said, doing his best to hide his confusion.

I got off the phone and walked into Paul's office.

'If you're serious about this Green Goddess thing we have two weeks to make up a range and we can test it at The Home Show.'

He looked at me and grinned his head off.

'You're on.'

The next two weeks were a fog of designing labels (thanks to my son Daniel), finding bottles, endless nights after work stirring and pouring and sticking on labels. By the end of it we had our range. Sixty bottles each of Wendyl's Green Goddess spray cleaner, glass cleaner, lavender laundry liquid, blueing powder and anti-bacterial spray.

We piled them all into the back of the Prius, rented an Eftpos machine and headed off to the Home Show with Pearl in tow to help out.

After three days of great sales and lots of interest we decided that we had a business and Wendyl's Green Goddess was born.

I got home and found that scruffy piece of paper with Deborah's wise words and framed it. As I write this it is on the wall above my desk, a reminder of a great idea, given to me by a patient woman, to stop me making a wrong turn. That's what I call true friendship.

Little did I know that six months later, I would trudge into my counsellor's office, dump a lovely calico recyclable Wendyl's Green Goddess bag full of products on her floor and, when she asked me why I had come to see her after two years, simply point at the bag and say: 'Bloody Green Goddess.'

Oat Bath

This is great for soothing inflammation,
like sunburn or rashes. You can just chuck
in a cupful of oats to your bath to get the skin healing
and soothing benefits and it leaves the water incredibly
soft. At the end you will have to scoop out all the oats
in the drain or you might clog it. To avoid having to do
this, you could get some muslin or old net curtains and
cut them into squares to make winter warming sachets
with these ingredients:

½ cup oatmeal

1 teaspoon ground allspice

½ teaspoon ground cardamom

½ teaspoon ground ginger

½ teaspoon ground cinnamon

6 cloves

Mix all the ingredients together. Either add them to
the bath as it is running or make a sachet by placing
the mixture in the middle of a piece of muslin. Tie the
ends of the muslin at the top with a ribbon or string
and throw in your bath about 10 minutes before you get
in. Use the bag to rub all over your skin and distribute
the wonderful spicy aromas.

Mulled-wine Bath

I love this recipe because you can save some and drink it while you soak in it! When I first told Paul this is what I intended to do he thought I was inviting him to drink the mulled wine once it had all been put in the bath. 'Yuck, I'm not drinking your bath dirt!' Needless to say we sorted it out and he loved drinking the wine while I bathed in it.

1 bottle strong, cheap red wine (a Merlot is good)

6 cloves

1 stick cinnamon

1 vanilla pod

2 star anise pods

peel of one orange

¼ teaspoon ground nutmeg

2 bay leaves (preferably fresh)

Put all the ingredients in a pot and bring to the boil. Turn the heat to low and let simmer with the lid on for 10 minutes. Be gentle. Take off the heat, add a cup to the bath and drink the rest!

Circulation Bath

If you feel that you need to get your feet and hands warm, run a hot bath and throw in a cupful of Epsom salts with 10 drops of eucalyptus oil. You will also benefit from the magnesium in the Epsom salts being absorbed into your bloodstream

Face Mask

A hot bath is the best place to use a face mask as it is often the only time you have some privacy. It is also the ideal place to sit still and relax to get the full benefit of the mask. Here are a couple of my favourites:

Yeast Mask

This mask brings out any impurities in the skin so don't plan a big night out immediately after you've used it as you may have a few blotches:

1 teaspoon honey

1 teaspoon brewer's yeast

1 teaspoon milk

1 teaspoon oil, such as olive or, even better, almond or avocado

Add a few drops of hot water to the honey to melt it slightly and then blend in the brewer's yeast. Add the milk to soften it and you should have a thick paste. Apply the oil to your face and then put the mask on. Leave on for half an hour and then remove with warm water.

Nourishing Mask

I like to use this if my skin feels a bit dried out by the cold weather.

1 tablespoon oatmeal

1 tablespoon almond meal (finely ground almonds)

About 1 tsp rosewater

Mix together the oatmeal and almond meal. Pour on enough rosewater to make a paste. Put on neck and face and leave for half an hour. Wash off and feel your new silky skin.

Hair Oil Treatment

The nicest thing you can do for your hair in the winter is throw some hot oil on it. The best oils to use are olive, almond or avocado. Heat some oil and absolutely saturate your hair in it. Cover it with plastic wrap and hop in the bath. Wash out with a good shampoo after half an hour or longer if you can manage it. I sometimes do this overnight, just don't use the plastic wrap and make sure you have an old towel covering your pillow.

Hair Rinses

I love a good rinse and the art of this is in the application. Pour the rinse into a large mug, lean over a basin with the plug in. Up-end the mug on the back of your head so that the rinse pours out slowly all through your scalp and hair. Collect up the rinse from the basin and pour it over your head again. Wrap a towel around your head and leave it on for 10 minutes or so before drying your hair.

Rosemary Hair Rinse

Cut several spikes off your rosemary bush (or find one locally that you can use), making sure to cut from the base of the spike so that you don't harm the plant. Fill a big jar (about 1-litre capacity) with the spikes – chop to size if necessary – and fill ⅔ of the jar with boiling water. Leave for 24 hours with the lid on and then top up the jar with cider vinegar. Use one cup at a time and enjoy soft, manageable hair. This rinse will last for about a week, but storing it in the refrigerator will help it last longer.

Lavender Rinse

Follow the instructions for rosemary but substitute lavender spikes.

Dandruff Soother

If you have a problem with dandruff or itchy scalp replace the water in the rinse recipe with vinegar, preferably cider vinegar. Heat gently on the stove in a pot before pouring it over the herbs. Proceed as directed for the rinse.

Castile Soap

470 ml water

170 grams lye (100% caustic soda or drain cleaner)

470 ml olive oil

400 grams solid coconut oil

675 grams vegetable shortening (Kremelta)

Make sure you are wearing protective goggles and gloves in case anything in this first process splashes.

In a large stainless steel or glass container mix the water and lye together. It will fizz and get quite hot.

Meanwhile heat the oils together over a low heat in a large enamel or stainless steel cooking pot. You want it to heat up to 38°C.

Watch the lye mixture and wait for it to come down to the same temperature (38°C). When they are both at the same temperature remove the oil from the heat and mix with the lye stirring constantly.

Eventually it will start to drag when pulling the spoon through. This means saponification has taken place. You will know you are there when the mixture is thick and the spoon leaves a channel that lasts a few seconds before filling up. This usually takes about 10 minutes but sometimes it takes longer. You can then add any essential oils, seeds or clay and pour into soap moulds. I just use plastic moulds you would store food in. Ice-cube trays work well for small soaps. Cover with a blanket or towels and leave for 24 hours. The soap should be hard and pop out of the moulds easily. If not, leave it for a few more days. You must then dry the soap out completely before use. I leave it for three to four weeks on wire baking racks to completely set and harden.

Hot Ginger Drink

5 ½ cups water

½ cup fresh ginger, peeled and sliced

1 stem lemongrass cut into pieces and bruised (thump it with the back of

  your carving knife)

1 cinnamon stick

4 cloves

2 tablespoons palm sugar

Put the water in a saucepan with all the other ingredients. Bring slowly to the boil and leave it to boil gently for five minutes. Strain through a sieve into a jug and serve hot. If you have a sweet tooth you might want to add more palm sugar or a dash of honey. Also a dash of whisky is really nice!

SEPTEMBER

ost people sum up their year on 1 January. I do it in September, because that is the official start of spring, even if it really doesn't start looking like spring until the end of the month. I start to notice the slightly longer days and experiment with wearing two layers instead of three.

I also get out and dig over the garden. This year I've given my main vege patch a rest over winter and planted a cover crop of blue lupins. I did this four years ago when I first turned the patch of lawn into a garden and I think it gave it a really good head start. The idea is that the lupins become a green manure crop that fixes nitrogen in the soil by dragging it up with their long root system as well as aerating the soil. Then you dig in the lupins before they flower. I love lupin flowers but if you let the whole lot flower you'll have issues with seed everywhere in the future so I let a select few produce their gorgeous spikes of blue/purple flower heads to bring inside for my vases and dig in the rest.

I also start off the tomato seeds that I saved from summer. First I plant them in tiny little plastic houses that I keep indoors before putting them in a warm spot on the front deck. I'm always amazed that these little seeds that have been sitting in an envelope in my seed box can spring back into life so abundantly.

There's not really much else to do until the weather warms up. I've made the mistake of planting out in September, enthusiastic as always, but everything just sits there and refuses to grow, waiting until the real spring arrives and the soil warms up in October.

During the year I have usually involved myself in a few mad fads for some reason or other. This year was no different. I drank a teaspoon of cinnamon a day for a month as I read that it was good at balancing sugar levels and could help weight loss. I just added it into my coffee and made a really nice tea out of it with honey, but like most fads, I got sick of it after two weeks.

Then there was the apple cider vinegar that Paul and I both got into. I read that it was good for weight loss, as well as a million other things, such as aiding digestion, providing potassium, cleansing the blood, helping the kidneys, and preventing urinary tract infections. The list goes on. If you are interested just type 'apple cider vinegar' into Google and you will find a huge following. We drank a teaspoon of cider vinegar in a small glass of water before meals and kept it up, for two weeks, until I decided that my first taste of the day had to be better than vinegar. A lot of people swear by it though, and if I'm ever a bit poorly and feeling unwell I will give myself a few days on it just to help clear things out.

When we returned from Mexico, I was a little grumpy that Paul wouldn't let me bring back a tortilla press. This is a metal contraption which you use to squash the dough into tortillas before cooking them.

I found one in Costa Rica after walking several miles into a dusty village that was home to little more than a couple of mangy dogs and a small grocery store.

'Too heavy,' Paul announced, haunted by memories of me lugging frying pans home from Belluno, two hours north of Venice, and hefting coffee pots home from Rome – both times attracting excess baggage fees.

'Don't care,' I fought back, by which time the woman who owned the store was doing her best to ignore what she could only assume to be two stroppy Americans off the hulking great ship that had just pulled up down the coast. I put it back and sulked. For the rest of the holiday.

When Paul and I travel I always moan about the heavy books he buys to bring home and he always complains about my cookware. When we got home I mourned my lost tortilla press, mainly because I wanted to cook tortillas like the ones we had eaten in Mexican cafes and restaurants. They're nothing like the ones you buy in the supermarket here so I went online and ordered a press and tracked down the special cornmeal they use which is called corn masa. Hundreds of years ago the Mexicans worked out that by boiling dried corn with lime (the mineral not the fruit) they could change the chemistry of the corn so that the nutrient niacin became digestable, thus making corn a complete protein. This is the reason for the different taste that I detected in the Mexican-made tortillas. I mixed up the masa corn, pressed it in my press and produced astonishingly good tortilla. I did this for a couple of weeks and then got bored.

'I knew that was going to happen,' said Paul. 'That's why

I didn't want to get charged extra baggage for it.'

'Ah, but it's always here now,' I said. 'Our little piece of Mexico.'

One day I am planning to have a full Mexican feast and I'll make a thousand tortillas. Just you wait and see.

I did bring back a wooden molinillo which I initially thought was a really cool wooden spoon. It is a feat of wood turning and is wonderful to look at with its decorations. I realised during my hunt for a tortilla press that it was actually used to whisk up Mexican hot chocolate so that it goes frothy. In Mexico they make special chocolate laced with chilli and spices which you melt in warm milk and whisk. Back home you have to be a bit inventive but my Mexican hot chocolate sessions were very popular for the usual length of time before I got bored – you guessed it . . . two weeks.

Stevia was my next enthusiasm and it is one that has lasted longer. It is a herb from South America that looks a bit like lemon balm or mint. It can be up to 300 times sweeter than sugar, and has no calories. You can buy it in some supermarkets and health shops as a white powder, or as a dried leaf. I'm sure it will soon turn up as an alternative to chemical artificial sweeteners as it has fewer health risks associated with it. I encourage anyone who is watching their weight or cannot tolerate sugar because of diabetes or other complaints to switch to stevia and stay away from aspartame or similar chemicals. I have never forgotten my brother using saccharin by the bucketload on his Weet-Bix when we were kids and developing these weird skin growths, like warts. As soon as he stopped using the sweetener they went away.

Even though these sweeteners are approved by government agencies, I don't trust the fact that they are essentially a chemical that my body wasn't designed to digest. On a recent visit to the States, I noticed that they were starting to put stevia in diet drinks, which is a great move forward. I also saw a study a few years back from the University of Texas Health Science Center, San Antonio, which looked at 1550 people over eight years and found that people only drinking diet soft drinks had a higher risk of obesity. This might be due to the fact that they rock up to McDonalds and order a Big Mac, fries and a diet Coke. Or it might be that artificial sweeteners create some other reaction in the body. I don't care, I just don't use them.

One of my favourite drinks in summer is gin and tonic, and I used to try to save calories by using diet tonic, which has artificial sweeteners 951 (aspartame) and 950 (acesulfame potassium). In order to avoid these, I invented my own tonic mix to go with gin and it's not bad. Some people like to add a bit more stevia as I don't have a very sweet tooth, but it's a nice, natural alternative.

I am attempting to grow my own stevia plant after a Facebook friend who I have never met sent me a cutting in the mail. I can't wait to harvest my own sweetener. Every time I see my little plant it makes me love social networking a little bit more.

By far the weirdest fad I had all year had nothing to do with food. I put myself on a cellphone diet. For a month I would not use my cellphone as a protest against two things – the ridiculously high cost we pay to use them, compared to other countries, and the terrible service you get when things go wrong.

I put the call into Vodafone to say my phone was no longer required using my stern, 'I've had enough' voice and was told that they would be charging me $160 for that privilege and their termination technicians were too busy to take my call and would call me back. It took them a week to cut it off, suggesting that perhaps cellphone diets were the new black.

I began the diet regardless, pretending my phone had been cut off and I immediately felt so much lighter, both in time gained and imagined financial savings. I could now leave the house without being interrupted by calls. I felt so wonderfully disconnected and free. I'm not sure when I became convinced that I had to be available to other people every hour of the day. It's not like I save lives or deliver babies or drugs so most people can wait a few hours for me to get back to them.

The perfectly nice phone that sits on my desk next to my computer, connected to a landline, got more use and I enjoyed its clarity of signal and resistance to cutting out during important phone calls. I realised that on a daily basis the majority of texts I used to get came from friends and were either to arrange lunch or began with: 'OMG you'll never guess . . . ' And we could do that by email much more effectively. The texts I sent were usually: 'Don't feel like walking' which was code to Paul that I've had a long lunch and it would be really nice if he picked me up. And the calls I got were mostly from Paul who likes to talk to me most hours of the day, my mother, my kids or old-fashioned clients who like to have a conversation rather than email. All of these things now happened on the landline, just like they used to, for free.

But there were rules:

1. I would not become a text bludger similar to those people who 'don't smoke' yet suddenly find the urge and cadge cigarettes all night.

2. If I needed Paul to pick me up I would assume that eventually he'd wonder where I was and would turn up to find me at the restaurant before dark. Or dawn. Or I could get off my arse and walk.

3. I would wear a watch again, so that I knew what time it was.

4. I would resist the urge to become predictably evangelical about my cellphone diet and encourage others to join my protest and organise a street march.
5. I reserved the right to stay on the diet for longer than a month – possibly for the rest of my lifetime.

I lasted the full month with only one slip, when I had to borrow a friend's cellphone to let Paul know where I was.

And then it was over. Now I spend about $10 a month with my phone on prepay and I hardly use it. The diet taught me that we waste so much money on phones because for some reason we believe that we have to be available to the world.

I find it interesting that nearly everyone, even those on low incomes, manage to find the extra $20 to $100 or more a month to have a cell phone and the extra $50 or more a month to have satellite television – something they hadn't even heard of 20 years ago. Imagine what would happen if instead of spending that money – up to $150 a month – on phones and TV, everyone spent that money on good, nutritious food, and on rejecting the chemicals and additives in their lives.

This year I have become more determined than ever not to become an all or nothing advocate especially as my ascent (or descent as some people may see it) into self-sufficiency and chemical-free living has become more than just a lifestyle decision. It is now one of the cornerstones by which I live and I feel very deeply about the steps I have taken. But that doesn't mean I will be campaigning for Greenpeace anytime soon or banning certain foods from my home, or insisting that every meal I cook for my guests is made out of whole grains. I am more aware than ever of the abundance of people who are saving the planet with their arrogant, self-righteous, exclusionary attitudes. I'm just happy if one person changes one thing about what they do. It might be cleaning your toilet with baking soda and vinegar, even if you continue to use commercial cleaning products for the rest of the house. Or planting a few salad greens in a bucket, even if you continue to buy the rest of your veges. Or rejecting one bag of chips because of its 25 flavouring additives, and opting for one with just three ingredients. In my experience once you start this process you begin to enjoy the power it gives you and the way it makes you feel both in the way your body responds and functions and the way your mind feels. But no one is going to change the way they live completely overnight and black and white thinking or shaming people out of acting in a certain way is not going to change anything.

If you go on Facebook you will find the one act of negativity I performed this year. I usually try to maintain good karma by following my mother's golden rule: If you haven't got anything nice to say, don't say anything at all. A rule I often flouted in the old days.

But if there's one thing I can't abide, it is bad service. Especially when it is in a health shop where many people will come in, having just changed one thing in their lives, but eager to learn more, perhaps after reading this book.

There is a health shop in my neighbourhood and I have never been there without feeling like I was a middle-aged white woman who was 'dabbling' in healthy living and had no idea what I was doing — which used to be very true. I used to put up with their attitude towards me and then something snapped one day after I had an experience in another type of health shop:

'It's cancer. Ovarian cancer. I'm riddled with it,' said the older woman behind me.

It's not something you expect to hear as you are idling away your time in a shop, but there it was. Out there.

She and I were the only customers in a shop that sells natural, organic beauty products. I was in seventh heaven, the other woman clearly wasn't. She was trying to find something to clear her sinuses, a product her husband later found next door at a book shop.

I knew all this because I'm a dreadful eavesdropper. Have been all my life.

The woman working in the shop had obviously sensed some tension in her voice, as did I, thinking that she had some pre-flight nerves going on. She invited her to have a seat and immediately started massaging her hands and neck, talking to her softly and that's when she came upon the lump on her neck.

'What's this?' she said.

And that's when three women in one shop felt the awkward silence that follows when someone says 'cancer' out loud. One of us was dying. I paused mid-examination of a lipstick, took a breath and closed my eyes. The woman with the lump said nothing and the woman giving the massage moved the conversation on deftly.

When her husband rejoined the silent woman, the massage giver set about making them both feel like they were the most interesting, most wonderful people she had ever met, massaging away, pressure points pressed.

'You two just have an energy about you. You have to tell me how you met,' she asked.

Ten minutes later I was on my second round of the shelves, unable to leave, unable to stop eavesdropping when the couple left waving fondly as if leaving a close relative, no longer the sad, tense duo who had arrived in the shop.

'You made her feel fantastic,' I said to the woman. 'That was so nice of you.'

She looked at me as if to say 'Who wouldn't?'

I got out my credit card and attempted to buy the entire contents of the shop.

Later that day I visited my local health shop. The one I have shopped at for 20 years despite always being made to feel inferior. On many occasions I have wanted to scream 'My sandals may not be made out of recycled tyres, and I may have washed my hair this month but I eat brown rice and I know what rejuvelac is!' just to wipe the smug looks off their faces.

'Could you help me please?' I asked the woman manning the naturopath end of the shop.

'I am mixing!' she replied sternly as if I had just interrupted an ancient ritual of witchlike proportions. What she was actually doing was putting some bottles away.

I moved off to wait. She answered the phone and chatted amiably.

I waited some more. Another woman hovered.

'She's busy,' I informed her.

Then another woman joined us. Three women in a shop. One of us might have been riddled with cancer.

'Not you, she's first,' the shop woman instructed as she signalled me to talk.

I told her what I was looking for.

'We don't have it,' she snapped.

'My friend bought it here yesterday.'

She stomped off, found it and thrust the bottle at me.

I didn't thank her. I drove home wondering how two shops selling products targeted at people who have either a genuine need or simply a desire to live a healthier, more healing, organic lifestyle could treat people so differently.

And then I went on Facebook and started a survivors' group for people that felt the same way as me about the store, which at time of writing has 50 members and many comments supporting my desire for better service from a shop which is there to heal people.

I knew it was a bad thing to do, to send out negative energy, but sometimes this peaceful, Zen-like being I have become reaches back into her dark recesses and stamps her big feet. At best it may have changed the way this shop looks at their customers as real people in need of help, rather than insignificant people who hand over wads of cash for highly-priced, hard to get wholefoods. On the other hand I've probably just stacked up a bit of bad karma to come back my way in the future. Hopefully my toxin load will be sufficiently low to be able to withstand it. The other negative is I don't shop there anymore, how could I? Which means I have to send Paul up with lists or drive halfway across town to find another shop that stocks my various health shop staples.

One friend told me that a week after I posted the page the entire staff were wearing T-shirts with my photo on them. I was shocked — until she confessed she was just having me on!

My friend Kerre was in there recently and asked one of the naturopaths to make up a bach-flower potion for a friend who was a bit stressed out and overloaded.

When the naturopath went to write on the bottle she asked for the woman's name.

'Wendyl,' said Kerre, as bold as brass.

'The Wendyl who started that group on Facebook?' she said.

'Yes, yes, but she does have a point,' said Kerre defending me to the hilt. 'There are some people in this store who need to take a good look at themselves,' she continued. 'Not you, of course,' she hastily added.

The naturopath wrote my name on the label and handed it over to Kerre.

'I'm giving this to you with extra love,' she said meaningfully. 'For Wendyl.'

When she gave me the bottle and recounted the story I was very touched. And the bach flowers helped tremendously as I battled to meet the deadline for this book.

As the year draws to a close we have become old hands at backyard poultry keeping. Our baby hen Matilda has grown into a beautiful Barred Plymouth Rock with black and white laced feathers, set off by a brilliant red comb. For a while I wondered if Matilda thought she was either a cat or a human because she had no desire to hang out with the hens. But eventually nature must have overcome nurture and she joined Marigold, Hillary and Yoko as one of the girls after several distressing hen fights as the new pecking order was determined. Our hens have given our urban family the chance to get a little closer to the reality of raising animals which then feed us. We've learned that keeping them healthy and letting them have sun, grass and the ability to range around our property freely is how all animals should be treated.

It has also made me realise that my dream of a small farm property up north or out west is a long way off. With our Wendyl's Green Goddess business taking off we could barely keep our small urban farm going let alone manage a larger one. I turned to Paul and told him the plans for a lifestyle property in the country were off. He looked relieved.

'I thought this was your dream? I thought you lived for nothing else?' he said glancing at the many pictures of potential dream country cottage cuties I had pinned up on my office wall as inspiration.

'Paul, we didn't even get around to painting the caravan roof this year we were so busy. How the hell would we have managed another property with fences and mowing and weeding and well, everything!'

'Good point,' he said. 'But we will get it one day. I promise.'

'Only when we're ready and we can look after the animals we get properly. We're not city farmers swanning in from Auckland for a bit of country air. We have to be the real deal.'

And the caravan is still at the camp, waiting for me. She *will* get her roof painted this summer, and I *will* make her new blue willow patterned curtains and buy some new sand-coloured linen to go with her gorgeous cupboards and sparkling lino.

There is a constancy about my caravan that keeps me going through the tough patches. When life gets a bit chaotic and out of control the caravan is always there waiting. For a few special days when Paul and I get away on our own and talk like mad to each other, drinking wine on the beach, watching the sun go down, so glad to have some time just for us. For the school holidays with Pearl, reading books, chatting about life and watching DVDs of BBC Jane Austen adaptations and escaping into town for a good shop when we're a bit bored. For summer with all our kids, calling in on their way south, or staying a few nights all crowding in together in the awning and a sea of tents. For seeing my parents in the next caravan, sharing meals and gossiping in a way we never find time to do up in the city with our busy lives. For being just alone. As I was when I started writing this book. Just me, the sea, the sand and that trusty Formica table. Bliss.

Hot Chocolate

2 cups whole milk — not low-fat if you want a really creamy result.

30 grams of the finest dark chocolate you can find — at least 70% cocoa.

seeds from ½ vanilla bean pod

¼ teaspoon chilli powder

¼ teaspoon cinnamon

pinch of salt

In a small saucepan mix together the milk, chocolate, vanilla seeds scraped out from the pod, chilli, cinnamon and salt and heat over a low heat, stirring until the chocolate has dissolved.

If you have a molinillo, froth by rubbing the handle between your hands as you would if you were lighting a fire with a stick and rubbing it on a piece of wood. Or just use a whisk to froth it up. Serve hot with a sprinkle of chilli and cinnamon on top.

G and T Mix

juice of 2 lemons

¼ teaspoon stevia powder

1 teaspoon honey

10 drops Angostura bitters

Mix all ingredients together and add to a litre of soda water. Use as a mixer for gin, or vodka. Sometimes I even use it with whisky and add more lemon juice for a whisky sour.

POSTSCRIPT

I couldn't leave you hanging about the part where I sit in my counsellor's office and point at the Wendyl's Green Goddess bag and say 'Bloody Green Goddess.' After this book was completed my cleaning products business really took off. I couldn't believe the wonderful small-business community we had joined. We had offers of help and advice from so many people who we'd never met before who sent us links for helpful websites, provided information, lent us books and were patient with us as we felt our way (especially Mark Stewart, our accountant). We finalised our bottles and label designs and I insisted that on each bottle we reprinted the recipe for people to make it themselves.

'But surely that will mean they won't buy it again and we'll have no sales growth,' argued Paul.

'I know that 80 per cent of my customers will continue

to buy and 20 per cent will make it themselves. And that makes me feel that my original reason for doing all this is having some impact. People are making their own cleaners, rejecting the chemicals in commercial cleaners and taking control of their homes,' I said.

'Where did you get that 80/20 figure?' asked Paul

'Out of my head. But I know it's right. And here's another thing out of my head. By printing the recipes people will know I'm not just selling these things to make a million dollars. It's just an extension of the message I'm trying to deliver.'

He wasn't convinced, but then I had a lunch with an old friend and advertising guru Mike Hutcheson who said one word: 'Trust'.

'And trust is the hardest thing to win from your customer in marketing terms,' said Mike.

So now every bottle goes out with the recipe on it, the ultimate driver to recycle and help my customers learn to live like a nana.

Eventually we were churning out hundreds of bottles from our kitchen, packing them off to hundreds of people and I was getting hundreds of emails from people wanting to know how to get stains off their sofas and what kind of soap to use in their laundry liquid. I had never intended the business to be this big so I handed the day-to-day running of it over to Paul who loved, and still loves, it. Every last bit of it. I struggled, though to deal with all the emails and keep up my usual workload of three weekly columns, a weekly newsletter, one monthly column and two radio slots a week plus the extra pressure of writing a book.

Then I started getting the grumpy messages. 'I emailed you three days ago and I still haven't heard from you. Please reply immediately or I will think you very rude.'

I was so tempted to write back and explain that I was getting hundreds of emails just like this every day, I was overwhelmed and please leave me alone, but I knew that this was part of the brand I had created — to be there for people, a believable person who was living a healthier life, rejecting chemicals and trying to help others do that too. But I was beginning to hate it. I just wanted my old life back where I pottered around my garden, experimented with natural recipes and wrote a few columns and books. Exactly the life I had described to my friend Deborah as being boring in August.

I went to my counsellor Gail Ratcliffe who I have seen for 18 years off and on, ever since Virginia died. I hadn't seen her for two years. I blurted out how much pressure I was under, how hard it was being a Green Goddess, how I wished it would all go away. We talked for an hour and I went home.

'How did it go?' asked Paul as he busily packed up another batch of send-outs of Wendyl's Green Goddess products.

'I think in counselling speak she gently took an hour to tell me to get over myself,' I said.

Paul smiled knowingly. 'Really?'

'Apparently I have a great husband, a good relationship, five healthy and happy kids, one blossoming grandchild, a successful writing career, a growing and soon to be successful business, no major financial worries and I'm in very good health.'

'I could have told you that,' he laughed.

'You know I never listen to you,' I smiled and gave him a huge hug.

By the time you read this I hope Wendyl's Green Goddess has grown according to the business plan Paul has developed for it. But I also hope that you, my reader, all the people who read my columns, newsletters, and listen to me on the radio have become part of a movement. To quote farmer Joel Salatin from *The Omnivore's Dilemma* by Michael Pollan:

'We don't need a law against McDonald's or a law against slaughterhouse abuse – we ask for too much salvation by legislation. All we need to do is empower individuals with the right philosophy and the right information to opt out en masse.'

I hope that by the time you have read this journal, a journey through a year of rejecting chemicals in beauty products, commercial cleaners and processed food that you might be part of my movement. The Green Goddess movement. We shouldn't rely on our government to pass laws to protect us, they are too prone to lobbyists from big industries and there's only so much the Green Party can do. Instead we need to educate ourselves and make our own decisions for not only our lives, but for those of our children and grandchildren. Opt out of what is killing us and opt in to living like a nana.

GREEN GODDESS TOP 20 RECIPES

Laundry Detergent

½ bar or 60 grams castile or vegetable-based or Sunlight soap, grated

1.5 litres of water

½ cup washing soda

¼ cup borax

1 litre hot water

Place soap in a saucepan with the first quantity of water and heat on low until soap is dissolved. Stir in washing soda and borax. Stir for a few minutes until thickened and remove from heat. (If you're using castile or vegetable-based soap it won't thicken straight away, but don't worry, it will thicken overnight in the bottles). Add 1 litre of hot water to a bucket. Add soap mixture and mix well. Fill bucket with another 5 litres of hot water and mix well. Pour into old milk bottles or other containers and set aside for 24 hours or until mixture thickens. Use half a cup of mixture per load of washing. It is easy to squeeze from the bottles as it is quite gluggy.

Tip: Add about 20 drops lavender oil at the end before pouring into the bottles for a nice fragrance or try eucalyptus oil, which is great for washing woollens.

Fabric Softener

I rarely bother with a fabric softener, but both vinegar and washing soda are great. Simply add ½ cup white vinegar to the rinse cycle, or add ½ cup washing soda to your wash to soften the water. Or make this softener:

1 cup washing soda

1 cup white vinegar

10 drops essential oil of your choice (e.g. lavender, lemon, eucalyptus)

Mix together and store in a bottle. Use as you would a commercial softener.

Spray Cleaner

This is easy to mix up and not only cleans well but fills the air with gorgeous smells. It takes a whole minute to make.

Nearly fill a I litre spray bottle with water. Add I teaspoon of baking soda, a few drops of liquid soap (preferably Dr Bronner's castile liquid soap, or use Sunlight) and IO drops of lavender or tea-tree essential oil. Shake together. If you have wooden bench tops, add about I teaspoon of olive oil and shake the bottle every time you use it to disperse the oil.

You can use other essential oils in the spray cleaner. In the winter I like to use warm oils, like cedarwood, rosemary, clove or even some natural vanilla essence, to give the kitchen a cosy smell. In summer, go for citrus smells like orange, lemon or lime. If flies are a problem use citronella oil which will help deter them.

Glass Cleaner

Fill a spray bottle with 2 cups water and I cup white vinegar. Add a few drops of liquid detergent and a few drops of lavender oil. Spray windows, wipe with a rag and finish off with scrunched up newspaper

Natural antibacterial spray

Many disinfectants on the market are highly toxic and too strong for the home. In the old days herbs were used to disinfect the home environment. Lavender, mint, lemon balm and thyme were laid on floors, hung from rafters and potted up in window boxes. This spray is great for using on your chopping board and any other areas you want to stay bacteria-free, such as sick rooms.

1 cup water

20 drops sweet orange essential oil

10 drops lavender essential oil

10 drops eucalyptus essential oil

Pour water into a spray bottle. Blend essential oils in a glass jar. With an eyedropper add 8 drops of this base to the spray bottle. Spray on surface and let set for at least 15 minutes. No need to rinse. Keep the base oil mix in a dark-coloured glass bottle in the cupboard and use to mix up more spray as you need it.

Tip: Use neat orange essentail oil to stop cats urinating in the same spot inside the house. Put it in a dish. Or, you can simply peel an orange and scatter the peel around.

Oven Cleaner

Cleaning ovens is potentially one of the most toxic things we do in our homes. Yet a mix of baking soda and washing soda can do the job for you.

Mix together one cup each of washing soda and baking soda. Sprinkle the bottom of the oven to cover. Spray with water until very damp, and keep moist by spraying every few hours. Let set overnight. In the morning scoop it all up along with the grime, and rinse.

If your oven is in a really bad way and has a lot of baked-on grime and grease, you may need to pour some vinegar over the washing soda. Let it fizz for 10 minutes then scrub with steel wool. Keep applying both the washing soda and the vinegar and scrubbing until all the grime has gone.

You won't get a headache from the fumes, or be polluting your house, but do wear rubber gloves as the washing soda can be quite tough on the hands.

Silver Cleaner

Cleaning silver has never been easier than when you use washing soda crystals.

You will need a container large enough to hold the item to be cleaned, preferably made of aluminium, such as a pot, pan or jam pan, etc. Alternatively, use enough aluminium foil to cover the bottom of a glass bowl.

Make a solution by mixing three teaspoons of washing soda per litre of hot water, mixing enough to cover the item to be cleaned. Immerse item to be cleaned, making sure that it is in contact with the aluminium when in the solution.

Lightly tarnished items should come clean in seconds, while heavily tarnished items may need repeat treatment and even the help of a soft-bristled paintbrush to help rub off the tarnish.

If you are cleaning a mass of cutlery in a stainless-steel sink or in some other stainless-steel container this will take longer, as the solution will first clean the stainless steel. It is the use of aluminium that sets off the cleaning action.

Rinse in clear water and dry with a soft cloth.

Warning: do not immerse any non-metal items or

items with painted surfaces, as damage could be caused. These could be items of jewellery, and be cautious if silver items have other non-silver components.

Floor Cleaners

Linoleum

I know very few people have linoleum anymore but I happen to have a 1968 caravan with some rather special retro lino that needs to know I love it. This brings up the pattern really well and I also use it on the veneer cupboards.

1 cup white vinegar

1 cup turpentine

½ cup raw linseed oil

Shake well, rub on with a cloth and then polish with a clean cloth. Shake bottle frequently.

Natural Floor Cleaner

This won't sparkle, and sometimes it leaves a few streaks, but it is great for all floors. The secret is to use a barely damp mop, not a soaking one. I like to use an old-fashioned rag mop, which can still be bought at hardware stores. I also carry around a shaker full of baking soda to sprinkle on any hard-to-shift spots as I go.

To 4 litres of hot water add a squirt of liquid soap (Sunlight or Dr Bronner's castile) and a cup of white vinegar. Add a good 10 drops of lavender essential oil, or any other kitchen oils that take your fancy, to give the room a nice smell and cut the initial slight vinegar odour.

Toilet Bowl Cleaner

Throw a cup of baking soda and a cup of white vinegar into the bowl and watch it explode. Leave for 10 minutes, then clean with a brush and flush. To finish, make a solution of 1 cup water to 30 drops tea-tree oil and spray all over the toilet, leaving it to sit there. Also spray on the outside of the toilet and give it a wipe with a damp cloth as bacteria lurk around there.

Toilet Bowl Stains

If you have a tough mineral stain that won't budge, you have two choices. Drain the bowl and rub with a paste of a tablespoon of borax and a little water. Leave as long as you can, then wipe off. Or simply put 1 cup of borax in the bowl and leave overnight. Finish off with the toilet brush and flush in the morning.

Shower Cleaner

In a one-litre spray bottle, mix together 500 ml of water and 500 ml of white vinegar. Spray on shower doors or anywhere there is soap scum and leave for five minutes, then wipe off. If there is a lot of build-up you can use straight vinegar combined with a lot of scrubbing with a steel wool pad.

Liquid Handwash

The texture takes a bit of getting used to as it's more jelly than smooth liquid. The glycerine in it is a fantastic moisturiser for your hands. I find using Dr Bronner's castile soap makes for a better blend, but Sunlight will make it cheaper for you.

250 ml boiling water

2 tablespoons Sunlight Soap, grated

2 teaspoons glycerine

2 teaspoons rosewater

10 drops rose essential oil (or any of your choice)

Add grated soap to boiling water, stir and then let sit for about ten minutes until it melts. Then stir in glycerine, rosewater and essential oil. When the mixture is smooth, pour while still warm into an empty soap dispenser bottle, as when cold it will set to a jelly and be hard to pour.

Mould and Mildew

We all battle with mould and mildew in our bathrooms, especially in humid Auckland where I live. But there are several things you can do to prevent a build-up. Sunlight — actual sunlight, not the soap this time — is an obvious tool, so let as much of it in as you can by opening windows and pulling curtains and blinds. Keep your shower door open to air it out, and encourage more air flow by keeping the bathroom door open when possible. By all means get a dehumidifier, but please run it on a timer, not all day. Do the same with your heated towel rail (which has nothing to do with mould and mildew prevention), but letting it run for a few hours a day after the busy shower time will dry the towels and also save on the power it would use if you let it run for 24 hours straight. Venting fans are another solution for humidity in bathrooms.

There is no need to rush off to the supermarket and buy a bottle full of bleach to spray all over your bathroom. Simply make a thick paste of baking soda and water and get scrubbing with a toothbrush in the grouting, or a good cloth if it is on the walls and ceilings. You can also mix the baking soda with a small amount of liquid soap if you prefer a soapier feel while you are scrubbing. Wipe off with a rag dipped in vinegar.

Mould and Mildew Preventers

Spray 1

Fill a spray bottle with 2 cups of water then add 20 drops each of lemon, lavender and tea-tree oil. Shake and spray where mould and mildew are likely to grow. Don't wipe or rinse off.

Spray 2

This removes mould from bathrooms and outside on wooden decks. Mix quarter of a teaspoon of oil of cloves into one litre of water. Just spray on and leave for as long as possible. Repeat if necessary.

General Purpose Carpet Cleaner

Mix two cups of water, with two tablespoons of white vinegar and two teaspoons of dishwashing liquid. Spray on stains, rub in and leave for 10 minutes or so before rinsing off. For tough stains simply pour on neat white vinegar and follow the same directions.

Milk Cleaner (for walls and vinyl)

Into a bucket of hot water add one cup of milk and one cup of kerosene. Rub on the walls, then wipe off.

Septic Tank Bacteria Booster

I always test recipes before recommending them but until I can afford my country farm I have no septic tank to try this on. Feel free to have a go, at your own risk, and if you find it useful let me know. If loaves of bread start growing out of your toilet, then I guess you should let me know about that as well!

500 gram brown sugar

2 x 8 gram packets of Edmonds Instant Dry Yeast

Mix together in a bucket and then pour on 4 cups of warm water. Stir and set aside until the yeast activates and you can smell it. You should also see lots of foam and cloudy activity. This will take about 10 minutes, maybe longer in cooler weather. Flush it down the toilet – this might take a few flushes to get it all down.

Drain Unblocker

Sprinkle two thirds of a cup of baking soda down the drain, followed by 200 ml white vinegar and leave for 10 minutes. It will form a gas that will clear the blockage. Flush with water. If there is still a blockage, repeat, but use washing soda instead of baking soda. Keep repeating until blockage clears.

Magic Night Cream

This uses apple cider vinegar, which has a great reputation for curing everything that ails you. My husband and I tried drinking it every day as a tonic and felt really good, once we got past the taste. A lot of people do this and say that it has a great effect on weight loss, rheumatism, and promoting blood circulation. Now that we don't drink it, I try to use it in salad dressings and I also like it in this face cream recipe:

½ cup olive oil (extra virgin if possible)

3 teaspoons apple cider vinegar

approximately 1 tablespoon water

3 drops lavender essential oil (optional)

Mix olive oil with apple cider vinegar. Add water slowly, mixing all the while, until a smooth white cream forms. If you don't want to smell like a salad dressing add the lavender oil. You will also need to shake it each night before applying, as it settles.

Lip Balm

This is a fantastic recipe and the balm is especially good for your lips with the addition of vitamin E oil, which also acts as a preservative.

20 ml sweet almond oil

½ teaspoon beeswax, grated, or cosmetic grade beeswax pellets

½ teaspoon cocoa butter

1 teaspoon icing sugar

1 capsule vitamin E

5 drops essential oil (sweet orange, rose and peppermint all work well)

Melt oil, beeswax and cocoa butter in a double boiler (or use a bowl sitting on a saucepan of gently boiling water, making sure the bottom of the bowl stays above the water). Add icing sugar and stir to dissolve. Take it off the heat and add vitamin E by piercing the capsule and pouring oil in. Add essential oils, stir and pour into a lip balm jar.

A Great Playdough Recipe

I've used this for years. Kids love it and it's really economical to make.

1 cup flour

½ cup salt

2 tablespoons vegetable oil

1 cup water

2 teaspoons cream of tartar

5 to 10 drops of food colouring depending on the colour intensity you

   want.

Mix all the ingredients together in a saucepan and heat until it thickens to a dough consistency. Let cool.

ACKNOWLEDGEMENTS

When I sat down to write this book I pulled from my bookshelf two books which I love and treasure and which I felt would help me find the inspiration to start writing. They were *Animal, Vegetable, Miracle* by Barbara Kingsolver and *The Kitchen Diaries* by Nigel Slater. It was only as I flicked to their title pages that I saw the hand-written inscriptions, 'All our love Catriona, Wally, Lily, Eva and Zema.' Catriona Peel and Wally Bartley are our friends in Sydney who taught me nine years ago the true meaning of good food, and how nothing gets in the way of a meal made with the best quality fresh, local ingredients. They made our brief time living in Sydney a joy and I would like to thank them for being the catalyst for so much change in me from the busy magazine editor they knew then to the Green Goddess I am now. And for all my beautiful books sent across the Tasman.

Thanks must also go to Dorothy Vinicombe, who really should be my agent, if we had such things in New Zealand. She suggests and directs my books with such skill and determination.

Many thanks to all my readers who have sent me emails of encouragement, stories of how they have changed their lives, and tips and recipes from their own nanas.

To our kids for always being so enthusiastic about the mad concoctions they have had to test, and the crazy mother they often find dishevelled but happily playing around with various powders and liquids in the kitchen.

Thanks also to my local community for their support. The Grey Lynn Amcal Pharmacy staff for always being so patient when I stumble in and ask them if they have any caustic soda or calcium chloride.

To the staff of my local hardware shop, Mitre 10 Ponsonby, for their patience as I search for drain cleaner, rat poison and for their great advice on the many home handyman tasks I have taken on.

To the Grey Lynn Library staff, who order me in strange books on request without looking sideways when I pick them up, who are patient when I lose them or return them late, and who often put books aside they think I'll be interested in.

Some of the material in this book is based on columns I wrote for the *Herald on Sunday*, *New Zealand Woman's Weekly* and *NZ Gardener* and I would like to thank the editors for their co-operation. An extra thank you to my good friend, Sido Kitchin, editor of *New Zealand Woman's Weekly* and Bill Francis at Newstalk ZB for supporting me and Wendyl's Green Goddess from the start.

To Judy, Bubs and Ian who look after my caravan when I'm not there and keep an eye on me when I'm down on my own writing.

And lastly, to the man who loves me whether I'm a crazed, driven magazine editor or a chilled out green goddess Nana: my husband, Paul Little.

FURTHER READING

Alice Waters and Chez Panisse: the romantic, impractical, often eccentric, ultimately brilliant making of a food revolution, Thomas McNamee, Penguin, 2007

Animal, Vegetable, Miracle: a year of food life, Barbara Kingsolver, Faber and Faber, 2008

Eat Smart, Stay Well, Susanna Lyle, David Bateman, 2010

Fast Food Nation, Eric Schlosser, Penguin, 2002

Flat Earth News, Nick Davies, Vintage, 2008

Food Rules: an eater's manual, Michael Pollan, Penguin, 2010

Healing with Whole Foods: Asian traditions and modern nutrition, Paul Pitchford, North Atlantic Books, 2003

In Defence of Food: an eater's manifesto, Michael Pollan, Penguin, 2009

Nourishing Traditions: the cookbook that challenges politically correct nutrition and the diet dictocrats, Sally Fallon. New Trends Publishing, 1999

The Aunt Daisy Cookbook, Barbara Basham, any edition old or new!

The Fragrant Pharmacy, Valerie Ann Worwood, Bantam Books, 1991

The Omnivore's Dilemma: a natural history of four meals, Michael Pollan, Penguin, 2006

Think Before You Swallow, Noel O'Hare, Penguin, 2007

GLOSSARY

baking soda — this is a slightly alkaline mineral made from soda ash. You can buy it in the supermarket but for the quantities you'll be needing get to a bulk food store and buy a kilo.

borax — this is an alkaline mineral which is a very effective antibacterial, fungicidal cleaning and bleaching agent, which is widely regarded as being better for the environment than bleach. It can be toxic in high doses and needs to be kept away from children and animals. I restrict its use where I can. It is valuable as an emulsifier, as a stain remover and deodoriser, and in the old days it was used to keep pests away. I only use it in recipes that won't touch the skin, as I have read that when it is mined it can become contaminated with arsenic.

castile soap — if you can afford it, I recommend this for all my recipes, however Sunlight (see below) works perfectly well. I use Dr Bronner's castile soap, both liquid and cake, because it is organic and fair trade and contains only natural, vegetable-derived ingredients. My website FAQ page has a list of suppliers — www.wendylsgreengoddess.co.nz

cream of tartar — this is made from grapes and is a by-product of wine making. After the grape juices ferment, the bottoms of the wine barrels or casks are scraped, for what will be packaged as cream of tartar. It is a primary ingredient in baking powder and is acidic.

essential oils — these are natural plant essences that have been extracted into oil. Unlike the synthetic perfumes added to commercial cleaners, natural essential oils not only add an amazing smell but have powerful aromatherapy properties as well as being anti-bacterial and anti-fungal. Never use them undiluted, and pregnant women should seek advice before using them. When buying essential oils check that they are labelled 100 per cent pure and natural and that they haven't been mixed with a base oil. For cleaning I mostly use tea-tree, eucalyptus and lavender, which are all relatively inexpensive.

glycerine (sometimes sold as glycerol) — this is a sweet, clear, viscous liquid that belongs to the alcohol family. It is a great old-fashioned stain remover used on its own. It has amazing moisturising properties as it is an humectant, which means it attracts water to the skin produced from animal or vegetable fats. Available at most supermarkets.

lemon juice — this is a great alternative to bleach, so if you have a lemon tree, juice a few lemons next time you need some bleaching power. Also slice one in half and rub it on anything that needs a major bacteria bust, like your chopping boards and work surfaces.

rosewater — is a by-product of the production of rose oil and is used in cooking, for perfume and it also has anti-bacterial and antiseptic properties. In Morocco they use it to wash their hands, dispensing it from gorgeous bottles.

Sunlight soap — I use this as a base for lots of my recipes. It is strictly not a brilliant choice for the environment, despite its old-fashioned values, as it is derived from animal fats and contains a few chemicals. These recipes use small amounts, however, and I reason that it is a huge reduction on the high doses of chemicals you would use if you used commercial cleaners.

white vinegar — this is very acidic and very historic, dating back to Babylon in 5000 BC, when it was used to disinfect and clean. For cleaning purposes, don't get fussy and buy the good stuff.

washing soda — I regard this as baking soda's bigger, tougher, gruntier brother, and it doesn't contain phosphates, enzymes or bleach. It is much more alkaline than its little brother and can be quite caustic, so wear rubber gloves when using it.

Appendices

Food numbers

If you are wanting to do a full analysis of the ingredients listed on a food product go to www.wikipedia.org and type in 'List of food additives, Codex Alimentarius'.

For a quicker idea of what you are looking at, here is a list of the category listings:

100-199	food colours
200-299	preservatives
300-399	anitoxidants, phosphates, and complexing agents
400-499	thickeners, gelling agents, phosphates, emulsifiers

500-599	salts and related compounds
600-699	flavour enhancers
700-899	not for human consumption
900-999	surface-coating agents, gases, sweeteners
1000-1399	miscellaneous
1400-1499	starch derivatives

A Checklist for Buying Cleaning Products

This list was adapted from one published at www.healthier-cleaning-products.com. Standards of green cleaning solutions that provide and promote the best health and well-being benefits to people include:

- Must be bio-based and contain no petrochemicals
- No petro-dyes (no added colours - blue, red, yellow, etc unless from natural sources)
- No artificial petro-perfumes (no added fragrances - pine, spice, mint, etc. unless provided by natural means such as essential oils)
- Non toxic to human or aquatic life
- Not corrosive to skin or eyes
- pH level between 2.5 and 11.5
- Does not contain chlorine bleach
- Does not contain ethylenediaminetetracetic acid (EDTA), or nitrolotriacetic acid (NTA)
- Does not contain phenolic compounds or glycol ether
- Is free of arsenic, cadmium, chromium, lead, mercury, nickel and selenium

Healthy Home Checklist

I've adapted this from a list provided by the American organisation the Environmental Working Group which is a non-profit, non-partisan research organisation dedicated to using the power of information to protect human health and the environment. You might like to sign up to get their tips and updates at www.ewg.org.

KITCHEN

- ☐ Do you cook with non-stick cookware? Replace with cast-iron, stainless steel or glass when possible. If you need to keep using it take care not to overheat it as it will release toxic fumes.
- ☐ Do you use plastic food containers? Use glass over plastic and never microwave food in plastic containers as it may leach toxic substances. Use glass or BPA-free plastic bottles for baby.
- ☐ Do you filter your tap water? If you're not sure what is in your local town water supply then it's best to filter it.
- ☐ Do you drink bottled water? Stop now. Buy a reusable water bottle, stainless steel is best and refill.
- ☐ Any canned food in your pantry? Try to cook with fresh or frozen whenever possible as some food cans are lined with bisphenol-A (BPA), a toxic chemical that leaches into food.
- ☐ Do you use iodised salt? You should. Iodine is necessary to maintain healthy thyroid function and is deficient in our soil.

BATHROOM

- [ ] Do you use air fresheners? Don't! Most contain a number of toxic chemicals that contaminate the air you breathe.
- [ ] Is there 'fragrance' listed as an ingredient in your personal care products? We don't know what's in 'fragrance', so it's safer to choose all fragrance-free personal-care products. Always check ingredient lists to be sure.
- [ ] What kind of toothpaste do you use? Choose fluoride-free for kids as they are prone to swallowing quite a lot of it while brushing. Also pick a paste without triclosan as there are concerns about how it reacts with the chlorine in water. Better still make up some tooth powder see page 191 for the recipe.
- [ ] Do you use liquid hand soap? If so, avoid anti-bacterials — the American Medical Association found that anti-bacterial soaps were no more effective in killing germs than normal soap and the anti-bacterial compounds used could contribute to the threat posed by antibiotic-resistant bacterial strains. It recommends against using them at home. You can make your own liquid hand soap very easily see page 281 for the recipe.
- [ ] Do you have extra products? Less is more. Not using cosmetics like hair spray and detangler, body sprays and powder is less toxic — and cheaper. Make your own so that you know what ingredients are in them.

LAUNDRY AND CLEANING CUPBOARD

☐ Are your cleaners green? It's hard to know without a full ingredient list, which most products don't have. Find out the ingredients by calling the manufacturer and if you don't know what something on the ingredients list is, ask them to tell you. Some green products will hide information behind loose terms such as 'surfactants'. Or make your own – the Green Goddess top 20 list is on page 274.

☐ Do your products labels list *all* ingredients? Most don't, but they should. Support companies that disclose all ingredients by buying their products – you have the right to know what is in the products you're buying.

☐ Do you need all those products? Most homes can be safely cleaned with a few non-toxic ingredients: vinegar (it's anti-bacterial) baking soda, water, microfibre mops and clothes – and some elbow grease! Skip the laundry products you don't need, like fabric softener and chlorine bleach.

ALL AROUND THE HOUSE

☐ Was your home built before 1978? If so, it probably contains lead paint. When repainting, use a wet sanding technique to reduce dust and have good air ventilation.

☐ Do you use compact fluorescent light bulbs? They contain mercury and should be handled and disposed of with care.

☐ Do you use pesticides or insecticides? Try non-toxic alternatives first; pesticides are a last resort. If you choose to use them, store them out of reach of children. Organic gardening is healthier for kids and pets, since they live closer to the ground.

☐ What materials are your kids' toys made from? Choosing non-toxic toys for young kids is especially important as they usually end up in your kids' mouths. Always buy toys from reputable manufacturers or, better still, buy ones made of all natural products. Things to be wary of are toys coloured using lead paint; soft plastic toys like rubber ducks that contain phthalates; toy jewellery that might contain chromium or lead; play make-up that is laden with chemicals – if you wouldn't wear it, why would you let your child?

INDEX

Babies and children

Beauty

Food